DELIRIUM

DELIRIUM

Robert Minhinnick

Seren is the book imprint of
Poetry Wales Press Ltd.
Suite 6, 4 Derwen Road, Bridgend, Wales, CF31 1LH

www.serenbooks.com
facebook.com/SerenBooks
twitter@SerenBooks

The right of Robert Minhinnick to be identified as
the author of this work has been asserted in accordance
with the Copyright, Designs and Patents Act, 1988.

ISBN: 9781781726723
Ebook: 9781781726730

A CIP record for this title is available from the British Library.

The publisher acknowledges the financial assistance of the Books
Council of Wales.

Cover: original artwork by Dan Llywelyn Hall

Printed in Bembo by Severn, Gloucester.

CONTENTS

Decima & Albert

The Magic Shop

I'm talking to Deci again. My turn forever now, making up stories, as she always told us stories when we went home for dinner.

"Remember HG Wells? Of course you do.

I chose the collected works, a set in red boards, one whole shelf from Albert's parents, but I always come back to the short stories. My latest favourite is 'The Magic Shop'. Just listen to this:

I had seen the Magic Shop from afar several times; I had passed it once or twice, a shop window of alluring little objects, magic balls, magic hens, wonderful cones, ventriloquist dolls, the material of the basket trick, packs of cards that LOOKED all right, and all that sort of thing, but never had I thought of going in until one day…

I think you'll love it and one day I'll read it all for you. Maybe it's because of what I do now, opening our little shop on winter mornings. Its porch is where people shelter.

Sometimes I have to clear up their vomit. And once it was human shit, not dog's.

People congregate in the bandstand. Gradually you learn some don't have homes. I know, I know…And sometimes when I unlock the door I swear I can smell cordite. Fanciful, you'd think? A whiff of battle come to our shop?

But there are six wooden chests there and branded on each, the words 'collate for destruction'. Each is zinc-lined and all stored howitzer cartridges on HMS Victorious in World War One, for which vessel, Robert Scott was flag captain. These six chests have the letters AE BROOM-FIELD burned into the lids, and the codings branded, secured by brass hasps.

And now, one hundred years later, we use them to store cushions and silks and dresses with tiny mirrors sewn into the fabric… those hasps fat as Babylonian dates, redgold and rusty under the palms, that palm grove beside the Euphrates where I paused and wondered, the dead fronds crackling under my feet, wandering the temple rooms where goats had shat their black pellets, goatbells the only music that was left in Babylon until the tanks arrived, and the soldiers discovered the demons that lined Procession Street…"

Feeding Porridge to my Mother
and telling her about the Deer

The agency nurse takes me to the agency chef. I explain that you're hungry, and it's the first time you have ever asked for more.

It's hot, I say, when I carry back the bowl to Room 19. Straight out of the saucepan. And I watch you blow on the first spoonful, but it's scalding, and I stir the bowl and stir the bowl until you can try again. And try again.

Half an hour later the porridge is gone. A whole panful with extra sugar and milk, and I realise I've spent thirty minutes telling you about the deer. Yesterday morning, I say. In driftwood light.

Suddenly, they were there, ghosting amongst the black-thorn, those trees themselves ghostlike at that hour. Maybe three. Maybe four roe deer.

Skulking?

Do you love that word? I do.

But no. In hiding. As ever, in hiding. Impenetrable I thought, that blackthorn wood, each tree a ghost, its thorns out of the sand, those thorns being spells and splinters, spills and spikes, and one still hot in my heel.

The does were chewing the blackthorn bark and were not expecting me, another ghost, but downwind, on the first morning in May. Three of them, and when they turned together those deer were spotted like vipers, or striped, I suppose, in perfect camouflage.

Yes, hidden, the deer. Out of hiding then vanishing into the blackthorn's dirty ivory, yellowed in this latest hurricane they're calling Storm Hannah.

Yes, deer, I say. Think of that. We don't often see deer in the dunes. And, of course I'll go again, but I don't believe the deer will still be there…

A History of Sunburn

Sometimes the visitor comes through the wall and sometimes the visitor is an animal and sometimes the visitor is someone she has seen or remembers from a past no-one else can share and sometimes the visitor has the wrong name and sometimes there is no-one there when she says the visitor has arrived and sometimes I look into her eyes and wonder who is this looking back at me...

❋

UV levels increase in the spring across the UK, reaching a peak in late June.

In this current spell of fine weather, we could see some of the highest UV levels ever recorded.

"Normally they're about six or seven in the summer months," says BBC Weather's Matt Taylor. "Today we

could hit a nine in some parts of southern England and South Wales."

BBC News for June 25, 2020

...while 75 years later I'm walking the lanes to Picton Court to verify how you are, recalling that you said Albert always kept a mouthful in his canteen, while the other soldiers finished every drop...

First thing I note is three of your friends out on the grass in straw hats, the nurses wearing orange masks. Not long ago, I could have told what villages those nurses come from.

But you're in bed and I'm talking through the double glazing and you're not hearing. We're all thinking of you, I say finally. Shouting love. Miming love.

Turning away.

Perhaps you hear me but I go back, past the horses we're told not to touch, and avoiding a woman coming in the opposite direction in her own mask.

Ah, sweet embraceable you! I want to say.

Am I the monster from your imagination, unmasked and anonymous, looming out of the honeysuckle?

Behind me stands Cefn Bryn on Gower.

I've always thought it my personal volcano,

its long eruption burying us in invisible ash.

They've cut the wheat, its stubble almost white, and sharp as limestone. My watch has stopped but this could be any hour in the last ten thousand years, and my mother is looking at the screen because Matt Taylor is speaking again, all about UV.

So I think of Albert in his own June, watching the cobra moving past the cookhouse, writing how ten weeks after VE Day

> *the Japs attacked last night.*

and one week later *the Welch suffered very heavy casualties …*

And on August 8, *Atomic bomb is used on Japan…*
a ghastly weapon this but should end the war quickly…

Then on Wednesday, August 14, he writes

> *peace in the world*

but one of the horses is wearing a fly-sheet to save it from sunburn, and soon my lips are crusted and my tongue flickering in the air like a snake.

Yet I keep thinking of Albert, twenty,
with mules and wireless, guarding his water ration,
and writing a diary for people he never thought about.
And I suppose that's exactly what history is,

> like my last sight of you, behind the glass,
> raising your hand and mouthing words
> impossible to hear…

*

Sun-burned, we come up from the orchid field, one thousand I'd say, no, make that two, surely, two thousand, that forest of coral spikes in the bleached grass.

And then as I am looking down, it appears exactly as I imagine it should.

At it always must. But my daydream is no delirium.

So there is no mirage, yet maybe an apparition.

But what I see is what I see, a creature erupting out of the hot and hollow earth.

And yes, I have a witness for this. I can call on her shared vision.

Some might say *dune tiger* or *rubies in the sand,* old-fashioned gemstones a child would scatter from the jewellery box, a grandmother's cairngorms perhaps.

Or even a cudgel of sorts, perhaps an amulet, but for me this is my coldblooded familiar, basking in its coils under the hemlock.

Yes, this is the basilisk, midday midsummer, mute, no malice, yet I skirt the serpent where it lies, deaf but squirming away, caustic, shrewd, from the echo of myself, the blood in my boots, the heart in my boots, the earthquakes it senses in every step, lidless, lethal, condemned to stare forever at disbelievers such as I, but both of us refugees from an eternal blood feud.

On June 12, 1945, Albert Minhinnick had written in his diary:

> *This is one of the worst*
> *malaria areas in the world.*
> *Also cholera. What a dump....*

This time I drive. And I am able to enter Room 17...

Yes. Me again. You know that shop where I work?

We're selling masks now, a woman is sewing them from her best material.

A real seamstress, I'd say. Have to look good for the plague, don't we?

Floral pattern all right? So try to put it on and maybe it will be a soldier who tests you. He or she will also be wearing a mask. But don't worry.

They will be as frightened as you, and as young as you once were, hearing the German bombs falling on Wind Street, Green Dragon Lane up to the Adam and Eve, and that one much nearer, close as the hayrick in Ty Mawr next door.

You were hiding, you always said, under the dinner table.

But who could believe the army rolling up the driveway into Picton Court?

They're testing for those golden stars on your screen that all the children are painting, gold and red and green that strange constellation suddenly visible in Room 17 and all around the world...

Gate of India

(Based on the 1945 diary of Private, then Corporal Albert Minhinnick)

Vipera

Twenty, wasn't he?
And in his diary for Tuesday, May 8, he wrote:
Heard peace has been declared in Europe.
Celebrations in evening. Bonfire and beer.
Had some fun.
Day off.

On Tuesday, July 2, he saw a five foot cobra killed with rifles and revolver. Full of snakes, he found the forest. If he cut one open there'd be another snake inside. A snake might swallow an even bigger snake. I know he thought about that, lighting up.

What was the worst one, then?

He considered a while.

Kraits, he said. The kraits were bad.

We'd been talking about how the other side hung microphones in the trees and taunted our side, also scorpions and the little tribal women who sold eggs and charged a packet of ten cigarettes for each egg. They were headhunters.

But my question was what any son would ask his father.

Did you ever kill anyone?

He looked at me and smiled.

Yes.

Yes?

Yes.

Yes!

He smiled again. And moved away.

Twenty, wasn't he? Now, I don't believe his answer.

I don't think he killed anybody. It doesn't fit with the man I knew, who kept a mouthful of water unswallowed when others were cursing thirst.

And dying of it.

But bullet or bayonet? Maybe he'd thrown a grenade?

Caught and tossed it back like a cricket ball.

They did that in films.

He left university knowing there were stories to write. Yet maybe he had. Killed someone.

A soldier on their side?

Because he never boasted or wore his medals, though hating their emperor, despising their jobs. But he was mysterious, this man.

Perhaps he had pulled the trigger on a lucky shot. Or bayonet practice saved his life. That man, emaciated in his demob suit, still to meet my mother.

Yes, dead skinny, bored with signal exchange, waiting for the parcel of cigs, and regarding the cobra by the cookhouse door. And now quick as his arm unfisted, two foot six, that arm unblued and unblemished from Mawchi to Mumbai, commando in the forgotten Fourteenth, no hate no love across knuckles or his clerk's fingers, radio man of whose autobiography in morse I could never get the hang.... But two foot six my own snake attuned to the reverb in my boots come out of the sand, golden my serpent with diamonds burnt diagonal on its back and delirium in each hollow fang, but moving as the knight moves on a chessboard – in slick dislocations.

And later he built walls around our house, hawks and floats his story then but never a mason's line with that mineral arithmetic and no blue chronicle or needleworker's lexicon his skin to prick, so maybe that was the clue to what made the corporal tick...

The Days after Hiroshima

January 22nd he wore tropical clothing the first time.
Then Sunday saw flying fish, Monday porpoises.

How much did he want to know? And what might he never tell? The answers could be somewhere in this tiny leather book bought in Motherwell.

But amongst the shitehawks on the ramparts at Rangoon he drank char in bucketfuls, wrote *nothing much changes here and there has been nothing very startling to record.*

In real ink, in pencil, the days after Hiroshima were days waiting for the parcel of Senior Service.

Oh, his parents had bought a new house. Incredibly life was going on without him. It's like what some of us call Face Book, old man.

He noted Thomas and Bond were in hospital with malaria, and whether from Cathedral Close or pisspoor Ysgwyddgwyn most of the boys also found they copped a dose of fevers and dreams, fevers and dreams.

His adam's apple wet, the black sweat-shine on the nape of his neck always the giveaways. That poison forever in his blood, but he never spoke of what had troubled him, apart from leeches and rain, leeches and rain, and once the hamadryad spitting from its hood before a sergeant discharged his revolver.

Quite a cushy life this, some chaps call it unemployment deluxe though at Kalaw a cup of tea cost four annas, while Venner, Larcombe and Green were dying in action just up the road.

So he brought his delirium back, every year the fevers and dreams, fevers and dreams of a businessman who hated business, and found neither twin would stay quiet in his arms.

So it was by motor cars we measured his life – blue Ford Consul, red Viva estate – with the paperwork across the passenger seat and all those disappointments in the home strait…

Glanllynfi

Yes, the usual smells especially in Fraser Street then the Dakota lifted his company east.

My one big wish is to get back to the old familiar things… But there was an acrobats' show he thought was good and that same night he bought a tin whistle…

On March 17 *How Green Was My Valley* was screened in the open air. It seems the Library of Congress considered the film should be preserved for future generations. Which means an incredible lie might persist.

Nineteen killed, the Welch heavy casualties.

But I think of him in the house on stilts trying to get a tune. He played by ear and no-one can teach that. Here's me clueless even on the black notes.

I don't know how long we are here but I won't mind staying for a while…

Now I understand where we came from, and where we're going. Our lives directed by John Ford. In a way Walter Pidgeon, Maureen O'Hara, Albert, me in my world of sand and crow garlic, the wind hectic in my head, my mother and the cockroaches are in the film together.

All creatures of coal, aren't we? Its seam runs through every vein, our lives fossil prints in the terrible carboniferous.

That typist he started chatting with had her own coal chores but not even the 2nd Battalion could defeat the black pats or mosquitoes he called monsoon flies.

Yet I think I can see those acrobats spinning through green light, a whole family somersaulting out of their own legend, and him on signals and the switchboard, the rules of mule training.

Soldiers like him were required for the Shan states, but it seems the new house had a breakfast room, a billiards room and trees he would write about in a story called 'the music of the crows', a chicken trained to stand on his shoulder.

Of all things the typist remembers that. But house, pub, restaurant? As if it had been decreed not a trace should remain…

That seam pitch black and amnesiac. These ghosts in the ink: lean boys in loincloths cartwheeling through X's of torchlight, a thin man smoking while rain runs down the thatch, mules braying in the dark, the chink of the balls, white against red.

But that shrunken head he saw hanging in the hut?

Of whom did it remind him…?

Plovers: February 28

(based on the 1945 diary of Albert Minhinnick)

Mule training, his diary says, and in this ice I see my father's playing cards, worn thin their sheen, and like his thumbs dark with nicotine, cards he carried through Suez, on the *HMT Maloja*, flying fish on the morning watch silvering to my own ideal of ice.

But there have been tomb raiders here, treasurer seekers, all those who have dug into this sand, because so many I suppose, over the centuries have been searching.

Now, here's February's last day, St Hilary's I hear. For me, the earth stiff and a pair of plovers, black and white their wings spinning spokes over the ice , white, black, laid out as a dinner service, plates and pipes of it, this ice, and now a snipe, single, though I search for its mate.

But Albert in Comilla explores the town, buys a tin whistle, stands to marvel at Chinese acrobats, in his war's first showbiz.

As for me on the beach this cold is blown bitter, and yet I can tell these dunes will shrug me off... as if... they've known far worse...

Cynghanedd

for Robert Hopes

Fathers?

Is this what they did? Built walls? Maybe around themselves?

But mine had an eye for stones and understood, yes, the souls of stones and the cynghanedd that stones demand.

No, not for Albert an exquisite jointing and pointing, but stones' mineral surfaces upon his palms, stones and stone dust and then how his wall might look and whether its line would read well.

So who were his walls for? Other builders, of course, those few privy to the language with an instinct for stones, builders who might scan and then reread and maybe memorise his wall and understand its baffling syntax, the harmonies they heard within his craft.

The Extinction Circus

The Extinction Circus

Don't know where it came from – must have pitched up overnight – but one little girl was selling tickets, under a sign for candyfloss...

So, having nothing better to do, a few of us turned up with our own sprogs, and that same little girl started going round on a burning wheel and there was an inflatable elephant and a boy with a tiger mask like you can see any day in B&M and everyone talking foreign-like whenever the music stopped.

What else? That knife thrower was good.
I was right behind his throwing arm. He had a spider's web tattooed on his elbow.

Blindfolded too, believe it or not, and I saw that same girl wince every time she felt the blade brush past her face.

Igor the Strongman had seen better days and there was one of those alpacas that are sometimes kept in a farmer's field, looking miserable. Fair enough, the kids thought it was great, and yeah, wasn't too pricey.

But today there's just a ring where the tent had stood, and these empty packets left in a ditch. And that burning wheel?

Seems it was just a hula hoop and now its plastic's melted all over the grass…

Rewilding

Aneirin in the Bay View arcade, Porthcawl

Bank holiday weekend. We're unused to the heat despite the year almost half gone. After rain, after cold, the sky is cloudless. Above us, swifts scream over the promenade. We soon find that the queue for the rides is too long and decide it will be easier in the arcades. The sign says we should use the hand sanitizer but the sanitizing machine is empty as is the bottle beside it. There is a sheaf of paper alongside the sanitizer on which we should write our names. Many already have. Many have not. I write nothing. Half way into his shift the boy in charge looks stunned.

Ahead of us the mother is about eighteen. There is a red Brythonic tattoo on her ankle that reaches her knee. As she turns I see it carries up her thigh. Behind her a young man pushes a buggy. Maybe he is twenty, unshaven and tattooed the length of his right arm. Behind him comes another young mother holding a screaming girl of maybe four. The child wears a marten-red teeshirt. This might be Dinogad. Behind the second mother waits another man of twenty, his arm and neck also tattooed, pouring coins into his pocket from one of the change machines. They are all playing *Monte Carlo*.

And I find I am staring at the first woman's thigh. Eventually three creatures become visible in the tattoos' swirls. The largest must be a *llewyn*, possibly a lynx, now to be reintroduced after extinction in Wales fifteen hundred years ago. The second might be a salmon, the third a deer.

Yes, she is carrying part of the chronicle. These must be the survivors of Catraeth, and I try to understand. My grandfather was billeted at Catterick in 1920, so a part of me was at Catraeth too, and I know I have a stake in this.

But I wonder which is the poet who will piece the *Gododdin* stories together, the nursery rhymes, the tweets, the media briefings. And I glance away from the two couples to the Covid steward. Even younger than these children, to me he looks as if he has taken something. Maybe *me-ow me-ow*. Coming down from it. But that is not to mean he will not remember…

Emily: An Algorithm

1.
Memory?
It's the first inheritance.
Also, the slipperiest deal we get.
But then it is taken away....

2.
I remember my daughter's friends coming to call for her before school. Sometimes they trooped inside and I would be suitably parental.
Got your books? I'd ask.
Yeah, they'd say.
Sure?
Yeah.
Homework?
Yeah.
Fags?

I remember their faces. Butter wouldn't…
I don't think schoolgirls smoke these days. Or do they? The lane behind this house was called Smokers' Alley. Maybe it still is. Smoking used to be cool. Perhaps it…

3.

All I had to do was type *earwax problems* into my computer and I would be inundated with solutions. Mechanical, chemical, psychological. I mean answers to a real problem. Because, I couldn't hear. Or only half hear. I was getting things wrong, you know? Mixed up. My daughter said earwax is the first sign of dementia. Can't remember how I cured it. Not the burning candle, anyway…

That was the first boulder in the avalanche. Didn't take long for the other solutions to problems to arrive. Constipation? Erectile dysfunction? Asthma? Anal itching? Itching all over? Memory loss? Dieting?
Look, in a long life I've had them all. You do, don't you? Come on.
But I remember one of those schoolgirls' faces. Joanne, she was called, as clear as day, we used to say. And how long has it been? Thirty, forty years? Memory, see. Yes, kind of slippery…. At least forty years since Joanne stood in the kitchen and I asked about her cigarettes. The face on her…

4.

Then all I did was type in *Emily Dickinson*. I wanted the *Collected Poems*. No, I wanted the *Complete Emily Dickinson*.

I think I've always liked her poetry. My mother it was who told me about her. How long ago was that? A century? No, but... Memory, see.

And all at once messages started to arrive. *The Complete Emily Dickinson*. Emily Dickinson's *Collected Poems*. Then *Selections* of Emily by umpteen other poets but not as famous as Emily Dickinson.

Yes, I learned to love those poems. Yet more important, I realized I'd always loved the *idea* of Emily Dickinson. That's why I didn't buy the biographies, which was how my mother learned of Emily's life. In fact, it was me who took the books out of the library for my mother. Several times. In those days when we had libraries.

They still come, those adverts for Emily. No, sorry, those exhortations for Emily, which is not a word I would use about the actual poet. Did Emily Dickinson ever *exhort*? Well, maybe...

One of the adverts was for *The Wisdom of Emily Dickinson*. Another, I think, was *A Poem for Each Day by Emily Dickinson*. I bought them both and that meant other offers arrived. The *Secret*... the *Mysterious*... the *Unknown*.... *The Recluse*... *A Woman in White*. You get the picture... But after a while it slowed down to one or two messages every week.

5.

And that's why I'm here, on what used to be the school playing fields. The school my daughter and her smoking friends attended. This school had been one of the first to install solar panels. Very modern and far sighted. As the temperature changed, the school made money from its solar energy. I would have liked to think they used those funds to buy books. Maybe the *Complete Emily*... At least one of the *Selecteds*.

Then a wind turbine was erected on the cricket pitch. Not so great. I always fancied myself as a leg spinner who could bat a bit. Summers spent trying to perfect my googly. Now, I can't recall how a googly should behave. Memory again... I tried all the pills.

Of course, nothing lasts forever. Twenty-five years the panels were guaranteed. Now, the roofs here are covered in glassy junk. Collared doves nest under those panels. As to the wind turbine, it has fifteen feet of sand in the hollow base. The vanes don't go round anymore. The turbine was controlled from Germany and the company went bust in the recession before last. Sometimes, the homeless sleep there, I hear it's comfortable on the drifted sand. You know they're homeless because they don't wear masks. The rest of us grew used to them years ago. The dune reaches half way up the inspection ladder.

6.

But, don't tell me about algorithms. They've followed me though life. It was an algorithm decreed that I should be the only passenger removed from an overbooked KLM aeroplane between Cardiff and Amsterdam. Ridiculous really, as I had connecting flights to catch to India.

There I was, with my bags, back in the booking hall. Stuck. But the airline offered another route, via a competitor, and that was how I found myself in Riyadh beside a golden fountain in the desert. And then on board an empty dream-liner flying further east. Surrounded by Sunni prayers over the intercom. The hilarious thing is, I arrived before everyone else for my meeting. Because of an algorithm. I think I've always been lucky. But it's wise not to panic.

7.

So, here goes. I take out my Emily Dickinson blisterpack. Like Amlodipine or Viagra or Atorvastatin or Asprin or vitamin B supplement or Diarreze or Diazepam. I paid on-line and the pills arrived. The driver had two children in the front seat of the electric cart. Skinny tykes but at least that system's still working. So much isn't. These four tablets are four little worlds that mean I will be able to write as Emily wrote. This is what the tablet allows. Fanciful?

It means the science of creative writing is over. That's what the advert says. The tablets are distilled from the proteins of Emily's inspiration. I owe this knowledge to an algorithm, and algorithms have led me well. They seem to follow me around.

The trick is trust. I recall circling the airport in Riyadh, late afternoon, before landing. Before I ever took off on the Dream-liner. Such a citadel I saw. What might Emily have said? *Blazing in gold and quenching in purple...* Yes, that's about right. And then the desert night fell, like the black stone of Mecca.

It's not a suicide pill, I'm certain of that. But everything's a risk. What might I say once I've taken it? And what might I write? I like the advert. Understated as was Emily herself, that woman in white. Usually....

Gorwelion

The View South from Cog y Brain

51°29'03.7"N 3°39'13.0"W
Grid Reference SS 85705 76884
Parish   Merthyr Mawr

1.

From Cog y Brain I can see another country and also look deeply into this one. In that other country sometimes the field shapes are revealed. In winter the snow will remain on that north-facing shore longer than upon the south-facing hills behind me. But now it's summer and with my eyeglass I'm looking south into what I think was the nuns' garden.

If there was a nunnery in these dunes it would have been inundated by sand, not least by the 1607 Bristol Channel tsunami. Yes, there are ruins, but these comprise a mill and a firing range. There are also huts and targets, and in Wig

Fach, large houses built for the sea view, south and west over Ynys Dysgr, one nearby house with what might be a helicopter landing platform.

But in my mind a nunnery stood amongst tiny gardens here in the dunes. Today I might take the path down through the sand towards the beach. The herbs I believe my nuns planted are the only evidence I need. By their colours I can list them, a melting psychedelic strata of blues and whites and creams and pinks. And lastly green. For me, these colours have sounds.

2.

Gorwelion today is more than a fanciful location on a limestone ridge named 'Cog y Brain'. It is a puzzling on-line community, the name of a computer game, a phone app, a dating app and a complicated series of drugs.

Some male members of that community have requested the game designers allow the on-line nuns to grow fly agaric mushrooms in their gardens. These provide the rage necessary to turn men into berserkers, capable of reaching the apocalyptic rage of the 'ultimate warrior'. The fly agaric, a cute spotted toadstool, like those once found in Super Mario games, is one of the main prizes in *Gorwelion*.

Woman on-line members insist that the nuns should grow all of the herbs used in the 'woman-of-flowers' myths, together with the edible herbs described by Shakespeare, Chaucer and Welsh language literature. Some of them have abandoned *Gorwelion* and created an alternative *Blodeuwedd* site.

Certain men counter this, insisting it is a human right to run berserk. This includes genocide, the slaughter of opposing forces, rape and pillage.

What constitutes *pillage* had always been a matter of debate. An Arts Council committee was created some years ago to define it. But simultaneously a media mogul advised by computer hackers and experimental chemists has created *Gorwelion*, an on-line game.

At the same time various drugs are now manufactured that supposedly provide the *Gorwelion* experience. Both sides claim victory. Those who sample the drugs claim them more profound than the game. Gamers disagree.

That strata of colour is present in the game, and I am informed, created vividly by the drug. Here is what I think I actually see:

3.

Cream – *Meadowsweet / Erwain*
Seasonally later than laburnum, this was grown to sweeten laundry and the stink of the privy. Also, to treat malaria, influenza, and any inflammation. It has been tried with Covid19 and its subsequent mutations. As malaria has returned to Wales with the changing climate, it is increasingly popular. I feel Duke Ellington would have approved meadowsweet.

White/Pink – *Yarrow / Mildail*
The first brewers and now our microbreweries have always valued yarrow. Sometimes henbane becomes an ingredient for careful brewers, with its heated seeds. Possibly Rimsky-Korsakov would enjoy yarrow.

Blue – *Ground Ivy / Eidral*
From where I stand I think ground ivy, a vivid blue, might recreate the old Welsh *eidral* beer. Possibly Franz Liszt would have favoured ground ivy.

Red – *Betony (Cribau San Ffraid)*
Not so common in the sands below but another possible beer herb. Yet Liszt might have rejected it, as he preferred the indigo end of the spectrum.

Pink – *Soapwort (Farewell Summer) / Sebonllys*
Its root and pink flower provide a useful lather. For dune detectives, another clue to an elusive nunnery. Possibly Liszt would feel more approving.

Green/Yellow – *Birthwort / Bara Hwch*
But maybe the reason people came to this desert is *birthwort*, or *bara hwch*, scarce and dangerous. Who arrived were swelling girls, with or without their mothers, but never the guilty boys.

Its poisonous fruit resembles gooseberries, while the flowers, strange cervix-shaped trumpets, ease delivery, or put an end to unwanted pregnancies. How often were such pregnancies the nuns' own? I wonder.

I think of those impossible children of the sand, nameless sprogs mewling like buzzards, bird-boned themselves. Skulls like wren's eggs. Little flutes nobody played. Only the nuns knew...

Richard Wagner might have appreciated birthwort.

4.

Meadowsweet was also used mythologically to create women of petals. Today, because of its anti-inflammatory qualities, it is viewed as an anger management treatment, a remedy for rage, for the 'red mist' that some men describe as necessary to become 'warrior-ready'.

On line, the nunnery under the sand is depicted as a low walled stable, with the nuns' luxuriant gardens divided into plots. It is visited by locals, (amongst them stereotypical yokels) and journeying pilgrims seeking help or wisdom as the result of a quest.

At the same time the nunnery is burnt and sacked, and the nuns raped and massacred by invaders who arrive sometimes from the sea or out of the dunes to the north. Exactly where I stand now.

Certain men believe such behaviour a human right. They claim it was once the norm and might be so again. These men point to our own history, with Lindisfarne, Iona and Llanilltud Fawr quoted as examples.

For them, the nuns practice witchcraft and black magic and are professional abortionists. In the USA, the Pro-Life movement has issued press statements to *Yo! Venice* and the *Miami Herald* after *Gorwelion* gaming machines were introduced. Possibly next year the Arts Council committee is due to publish its definition of what might and what might not constitute *pillage*.

Thanks for Riding

I thought maybe I had an hour. So I visited the allotment. Really, the excuse was to stand under my nine foot tall sunflower and breathe in the mist. And then dig some marris piper, pick a few raspberries in that remote corner.... Tropical, already somehow. And yes, weary…

And then the fairground with the grandchildren. Apparitions of my blood. Unknowing and uncaring ghosts of myself. Vanished into the melee.

3pm and filling up, and we decide on the Waltzer. Expensive, I think, and few wearing masks as everyone is requested. After a while, we give up bothering. There seem many police around, the word being a gentleman has gone missing from his care home.

The music they are pumping through is foreign to me, remixes of the already remixed. Thank God, I think, when Mustang Sally comes on. A live version, the bass shuddering through the floor and I imagine the bass player's fingers as the cars start bucking and spinning and the afternoon is now quickly feverish in the fairground's toxic draft.

And I look again. And again. Oh yes, I seek him out, the man who rides the Waltzer, the man in charge of the whole shebang, the man who chains us in and steps away over a gleaming metal floor.

Nippy, I think. Exulting in his own professionalism. And yes, *he looks like Lexington*. Yes. *Lex*. My year at school. Fifty years ago. Hardly ever spoke to him. Different crowd, different bus. *Lexi*. Different class, I suppose. But I recall the English class and once turning around and rolling my eyes, and Lex rolling his eyes in corroboration from behind the long desk. Or so I thought.

But now, I consider, and it comes in a flash, Lex didn't mean *In Parenthesis* was difficult. Or perplexing. What he meant was I didn't get it. Did I? His rolling eyes meaning to put me in my place. Who didn't get fusilier Jones in the briars of Mametz. And now two hundred yards away is a street called Clos Mametz.

That was before I moved here. Before I had ever heard of the surfing crowd. But if it is Lex, if it is my old English A level companion, he is still my age yet dancing on roofs of water, stepping between the cars that rotate and rock on three different levels at once as the music rises enormous out of the ground.

I had put on a clean shirt for the fair and changed my jeans. But Lex, if it is Lex, and after fifty years it might be him, is wearing my ripped strides with the knees pale and bulbous, my pink teeshirt with its broken neck.... And not for Lexington the proclamation of STAFF on the back of this but the threadbare livery of a workingman at the top of his game. Who has learned his skills through practice.

And I'd say cool. Whoever it is, he looks cool. And cool comes from an era when I never said cool. Never knew what cool meant but I thought I knew what cool looked like and I'm still staring as everyone has been told to look, everyone told to take off their masks and reveal themselves as not the lost wanderer who of course is not lost any more than any of us is lost but is looking as I am looking for the one familiar face that will make sense of any of this...

The Lapwing

*In memory of Caryl Ward, who told me about
the world of Bryn Cwtyn*

1.
Exploring alone
I come upon the lion of Babylon
with its curious basalt smile.
After nearly three thousand years
I see it now in the weeds,
sand covering its pedestal.

We are not unlike
the slave it devours,
an Assyrian snared
in the grass,

that sacrificial child
by death defiled.

2.

Burning photographs creates ash different from burn-ing driftwood. Here's one of myself. Smartly dressed and knowing it. The snapshot curls up in the brick-built bar-becue and disappears. Thousands, there must be, of special moments like this. Sixty years of hoarding…

3.

People say this is how you catch it. On public transport. The second bus drops me somewhere I have never alighted before. Ford's factory is scheduled to close with predictions of local catastrophe. The stop is half a mile away but it is thought the sales room and its garage will survive. At least, for the foreseeable…

Another disaster is the failure of the battery plant to start operations. The developer is going elsewhere. The site is already cleared but not the felled oaks. There are piles of sawdust in the tyre tracks that lead across the fields. Machines have already torn up the hedges.

But the showroom is immaculate as ever. I find my way through the ranks of cars on sale and past a man polish-ing a chassis. I can see my vehicle isolated in a special bay, and yes, I haven't dreamed it, still loaded with boxes and bags.

Inside Ford's automatic doors is the usual hygiene station with bales of blue paper toweling. I straighten my mask, walk down the aisle that demands '*cadwch eich pellter*', pause, and wait until a young woman beckons me to the counter. On her blouse is a badge. *Ceridwen*.

I note her fingernails. Two inches long. Vermillion. Like those of Babylonian astronomers who predicted the future. Had they ever glimpsed us?

Hello, she says.

Shwmae, I say.

Pardon?

There's me getting it wrong, again, I say.

First customer today, she says. Might you spell your name? Mm. Your total is £95 exactly. The tow comes free.

I mean my diagnosis, I say. Good job I'm not a doctor.

Mm?

Thought it was the starter motor. I was sure.

Will it be debit or credit card?

See, I remember how it used to be.

Debit it is, then.

When it was the starter motor playing up, I'd find a hammer. Or a big spanner.

Yes, £95…

All it used to take was a smart rap on the starter. You know, small hammer or big spanner. And you didn't require all the rest. Of it.

Visa'll do nicely.

But it was the battery. Wasn't it?

Was it?

Well, seems so. Don't make me doubt Kevin now. He got it working pretty well, he said on the phone. Batteries, eh? Pity about...

Kevin?

Pleasant bloke. Considering.

Considering?

All the incon. And the buses. Haven't been on a bus for ages. Nobody else on it. Apart from the driver.

Of course.

Nice woman. Told me where to get off. If you know what I mean.

I'll try this again.

See, it was urgent. We were clearing the house. The family house. A hundred years old it is. *West View*, it's called, but nobody knows that now. Forgotten. And I'd taken all the bags and boxes of books out to the car. Filled it pretty full. And curtains. Cupboards full of curtains. Long gold curtains, these. Pretty fancy, you'd think, and yeah, maybe they are.

Oh yes?

But then it was time to go to the medical centre. My injection. First one. So, urgent. Couldn't miss that, could I? But when I turned the ignition...*nothing*. Kept trying because I didn't want to be late for the jab.

Mm...

Terrible round here, isn't it? So many dead. Who'd have thought? Hundreds and hundreds. All around here. Well,

I must have tried ten times but I knew. You always know, don't you? That it's not going to be your day. And there was no time for me to find one. A little hammer or a big spanner and get under the car and tap the starter motor.

I wanted to try what I knew, see. But all the tools were in the boot. Under the books. Under the catalogues and all this gay porn and these pictures and magazines because the new people have said they want to be in next Friday and the house has to be cleared. First time *West View* has ever been sold in its history. Built specially see, for the family and passed down the generations. Very rare that must be. Built in that pandemic, you know. Spanish flu. Yeah, that other one. Apparently there's been interviews with people who remember it.

Ceridwen keeps smiling. I'm looking at her fingernails on the keyboard and wondering how she does it. There is nobody else waiting to pay.

So, what happened, I say, is that me trying to start the engine so often just drained the battery. Juice must have been low already. Had to have a lift, didn't I, from my brother-in-law. Told you it was the family home. Just in time too at the medical centre…

Mm…

Astrazeneca, that one. Don't know what we'll do next year. They should combine it with the flu jab, that's what I think. All these weird variants? We'll be like pincushions soon.

Working now.

That's a relief. As I haven't brought cash. So, I told Kevin about my theory but he never said anything. Probably before his time.

Kevin?

Works for you.

And your receipt.

Great to be mobile again. But now, here's the problem. All these bags of books in the car. Great heavy things, some of them. Coffee table type. Princess Margaret, Princess Di, course. And bibles. All these bibles. But how many bibles do you need? We've already saved the family bible with all the family tree written in. People I've never heard of. And all the Welsh…I never knew. Black, of course. Bible-black, as they say. Huge heavy thing. Metal clasps.

All done.

So, now I'll have to put the books in our shed. Everything that's in the car. Could get damp, I'm afraid because those books are immaculate. But all the second hand shops are closed down. And the house clearance people don't want to know until the vaccines make a difference. It'll be like our archive, a family archive. Only down in the shed.

But thinking of Ceridwen's fingernails, I remember again those astronomers cutting their cuneiform into clay. Because that was their archive. All Ceridwen has to do is tap a key and there is my service record. Omens and magic made the scribes famous. Predictions and scaremongering. Soothsayers stroking their square Babylonian beards.

Predicted the flood, didn't they? Like in the bible. But it's always been marshy around here, at Ford's, where the Ewenni river meets the Ogmore river and the ground is usually wet. Just think of all the farms that have vanished. *Bryn Cwtyn*, that's the one I remember. Those farmers understood flooding, yet now it's a tragedy every year...

But they named a street after it, which is good. Now no-one cannot say they don't know what *Cwtyn* means. *Lapwing*, isn't it? Some say different but for me, it's hill of the lapwing, even though it was never written down, apart from the deeds and on the farm gate. And now the street sign on the wall and in estate agents' windows. At least, that's been saved, and, yes, they had to destroy Bryn Cwtyn to save the lapwing. Funny that...

And now I'm sifting the photos again and considering the bibles. Ash in my throat, ash in the air but better not burn the bibles. What's that, then? Superstition? All the second hand shops closed and there's no space anymore.

OK, another copy of *Bent* can go into the hereafter and another Majorca album with those men so proud of their gorgeous tans.... All that extinct sunshine....

The Fairy Buoy

1.

You hear it before you see it. If you ever see it. Yellow, rocking on the swell. Like something made from Lego. Or a mock up of a single molecule.

A bell, I always   thought. A funeral bell, tolling in the dawn. In the dark, a yellow buoy with FAIRY written on it.

If you're in a small boat you can read the writing on the buoy. And hear the sound it makes. Yes, a funeral bell, that idea came to me once. Years ago. A muffled chime, warning whoever heard it to be careful....

2.

I think we drove east and behind us the buoy's music was lost. I recall a car park and an almost deserted beach. There was a cave ahead behind a waterfall. The pebbles here were slippery and I was thinking about why?

Two high tides every day, weren't there? Call it 750 tides each year. So how many was that over one hundred thousand years? Seven hundred and fifty million? Or seven hundred and.... But why one hundred thousand years? And for how long had there been tides?

I told you, my father whispered, bending over me. *I told you.*

He might have been crying. It was painful to see my father's cry. Worse than my own pain.

Let's see, let's see.... Try to smile. Try to smile.... Oh my God, Oh my God... No, it's not too bad maybe. But oh my God. You've ruined yourself. You've ruined... But not too bad... We'll take you, we'll take you....

The emergency dentist was Dr McHugh. His accent surprised me. I'd never heard a voice like that in real life.

Maybe there's an exposed nerve, said his Scottish voice. Does it hurt? I think it must hurt...

Maybe 730 high tides, I thought. Every year. Times, say, one hundred thousand. That was long enough. Surely, to explain everything...

3.

Twenty-one thousand and nine hundred high tides in our ocean later I sit outside in Yr Harbwr. A new bar and restaurant. Same coast, about fifteen miles west. I haven't come far, have I? Look, there's the lighthouse that fascinated us. Not far from the cave. Same time, I think. Late afternoon, the light's thickening pixels. Tide coming in and the rocks that built the harbour distinct and still wet. Gleaming.

All harbours are mouths, I suppose. Maybe *maw* a better word. *The jaws or throat of a voracious animal* the OED defines it. There's a bouquet on the quayside in memory of a young man who broke his back diving off these rocks. The deadly boulders. But it doesn't stop the children diving. Across the bay the neon in the funfair is a little brighter now. The funfair music blows in and vanishes and returns again…. Still Elvis. *We can't go on together….*

Someone taps me on the shoulder and I look up into the sun. Not sure who it might be but it's a woman and she leans down to kiss me, which surprises.

Isn't kissing forbidden now? A few customers at Yr Harbwr are wearing masks and I thought we are keeping our distance…. I think I return the kiss…. How could I not?

Long time, she says. *Long time.*

I glance past her at the boulders in the quay, gleaming. And suddenly the music isn't there anymore. I move my hand towards my icy glass and remember its chill but I do not touch it because I feel my mouth fill with something I try not to swallow. Not blood nor bile but my teeth that made my father cry and Dr McHugh shake his head. Because my precious teeth fall out of my life forever and on to the floor to lie beside the plastic bouquet left for the broken-backed boy.

In the men's urinal is a sign that stipulates one person only to piss at a time and one person only at the sink at a time and I look at myself in the mirror and smile and smile as my father instructed and I wait for the blood to arrive but there is none only a haemorrhage of memories which might be dreams or the fairground deliriums that have always haunted me in this place.

Then I step away from the glass but do not return to my seat or the woman I believe I kissed but walk from Yr Harbwr towards the funfair. Yes, the light is thickening and the music is clearer and it's still Elvis singing *we're caught in a trap…* and there are queues for the penny falls and the helter skelter and behind me another child jumps off the quay, arms around his knees. Twenty feet. The most natural thing.

But when I turn the corner it is another twenty-one thousand and nine hundred high tides later and all the lighthouses down the coast are lit or they might be beacons and the Fairy Buoy is ringing as it has always rung but is in a different position than I remember and there are new measurements on the harbour walls and the bars and restaurants are closed and the people I pass are wearing masks and some have plastic visors and gloves and I am also wearing a mask and there are others who say they are invoking the Riot Act and others saying too late too late, and a boat is leaving the harbour, the deadly boulders of the harbour walls, and so many have climbed upon the boat, hundreds it must be, pointing away, away from the floods, and there are people camped on the highest dunes.

Those on board had first sailed from Bristol. Their ship is The Balmoral. It was still burning diesel, some of the people on board were choking and many already seasick. Can you imagine hundreds of people seasick together?

America was still the word, on the dock and then on board. *America.*

America? Fools, I thought. Seven hundred tonnes, the old Balmoral. And what do two thousand people weigh?

I could remember the ship myself. I'd crossed to Ilfracombe on it. It was old even then. There had been some original fittings left on board, brass, the teak newels.... But people have started lighting fires on deck...

Now I ask myself, a very old man now who remembers his father and his father's father, who arrived from different places, how can we be refugees in our own country?

And when I understand the answer I realize it's been clear all the time... And I listen to the Fairy Buoy, rocking on the swell. Its hollow chime...

from Billionaires' Shortbread

Ffrez: Fever

Ffresni was stirring a pot.

House, she breathed.

Horse.

Hearse.

What? said Sparkle.

Three notes. For me to remember. Just three. House, horse, hearse. For my music. My little tune.

Oh.

That's how I write sometimes, said Ffresni, leaning in. Now breathe on me.

Why?

I want to smell your breath.

Oh.

Yeah. It stinks.

Bet we all stink, said the girl.

What would they think? asked Ffresni.

Who think?

Ffresni paused. The people in the sand, she said eventually. In the burrows. In the... *tumuli*. What would they think of what we have done to their world?

What people?

The people buried in these dunes. They were discovered in the first excavations. Hundred odd years ago that was. But there are more of them undiscovered...

How long ago was that?

Say three thousand years. Give or take...

Oh...

Clean as whistles, those bones. Children's bones, maybe. But all the people were small. There was one internment with two skeletons. One tomb. Close together, that couple. They might have been kissing. One arm over the other one. Kissing at the end.... And then slowly the sand rubbing them clean.... What's my tune?

Um... Horse...

House. Horse. Hearse. Three notes. Three sounds. Yeah, we all stink, smiled Ffrez. But today you more than most. Got your chewsticks...?

Nah...

I'll get you some. I think that dogwood works.

Ffrez poured some of the mixture into a bowl. She tasted it and shrugged to herself. Then tasted again. The infusion was green and there were flowerheads within it, flowerdust and shredded leaves. Her fingers smelled of those leaves, a goaty aroma. But the flowers had been something different, honey over her own hands. Wild honey she thought, and the prehistoric names of the flowers said the same. Yes, musk, a sexy perfume, an intoxicant it was claimed. Those flowers had been a scattering of stars in her lap as she sat at the edge of the slack and dug the root out of the sand. The flowers were growing in what was often flooded ground. But it hadn't rained for two months and the spring was dry.

She had sat hidden where apple branches met long grass. Ffrez didn't want to walk across the exposed depression. Six months earlier this had been a lake, the spring creating a river that filled the slacks and flowed on to the beach. Impossible to imagine now, she told herself from her place in the yellow grass. There were apples above her, red and wormy, yet fruit that might be used.

It was a hot day and as she squinted through the grass she felt herself nodding. Nodding and her mind wandering. Ffresni might have slept a few seconds, the meadowsweet in her hands, its luxuriance on her skin. Wear some in your knickers, then, she found herself saying. Like *seafoam* she thought, starting up from her drowse. And another word, another word that she recalled from ages past, out of the bronze age, the age of megaliths. Because a woman had been woven from meadowsweet, a woman who would not comply. A woman who did not obey.

But not a queen. No, never one of those. A woman who had sat beneath an apple tree and looked at the fruit, a woman who had tasted the cankered apple. The sand was hot under the grass but the flowers grew where they had always grown. Out of the sand the meadowsweet appeared where the children had been discovered. Or the parents of those children, so slight they were, their bones all laid in the same direction, the crouched dead, waiting to spring. Four of them, weren't there? Four buried here with love beside a freshwater lake. Yet she could hear the tide one hundred yards away, scent its salt. Then she stirred, tasting the sweat in her thin moustache, hearing the mosquitos singing...

Meadowsweet had been used on the floors of bedchambers, she'd read. A strewing herb it was called. Also to flavour wine and mead, or stored amongst new washing. And now she was using it as medicine. Strewing and stewing, she thought, its plumes like the tails of golden retrievers. But there were different dogs now.

Fucking horrible, said Sparkle.

Drink it.

No.

Drink it, you fool.

No.

Trust me.

Just weeds. Looks like compost.

Take asprin, wouldn't you?

Yeah.

This is just as good. Drink it.

The girl sipped again. Ffresni placed her hand on Sparkle's brow and shrugged.

Feverish, aren't you?

Yeah, doctor. Got a fever. I already know I got a fever.

The old man had the same fever, said Ffresni. Couple of the others.

So..?

So take this medicine.

My bloody head aches....

Yeah, you're hot.

Sweating, said Sparkle. I can feel it trickling down the crack of my arse.

But she sipped again and finished the bowl. Immediately Ffrez refilled it and Sparkle took a breath and drained it.

Christ, she breathed.

Look, it won't kill you. That's a promise. And it might help keep you alive.

Vile.

More later.

Vilest thing. What are you, a witch?

Ffrez wound a strand of the girl's hair around her own finger. Greasy, that hair. Stiff with wind and salt.

Maybe, she said. But witches are important...

Bastard potions, said Sparkle, wiping her mouth.

Yeah. Potions and spells. But spells are real. This spell might work.

Elmet had this fever.

Think he brought it with him off the ship, said Ffresni. Think he's always had it. Some people do. It's in their blood. The old man had it years ago. Off and on…

And Tiptoe, said Sparkle. He had it. Before he drowned.

Worked for Elmet, said Ffresni. Doesn't bring him down. Gives him dreams. Cai's never had it. But look, most of us have this fever. Just some worse than others…

I'm worse today.

Tomorrow you might be better.

Who says?

Know what it is?

No.

Ffresni poured the last of the infusion into the bowl. She looked at the stains on her palms. Sap's black milk.

It's not magic, she said.

No?

But it might be. I could have picked something to boil a gun flint in…

What's a gun flint?

Old firing mechanism.

Why would you do that?

Make the gun fire better.

Crazy.

Yeah. Maybe crazy. But that's what people did.

Maybe not crazy, you mean?

No.

Old times?

Yes. Old wisdom.

OK. Maybe not crazy. But this headache is real.

Maybe magic's real. But so's malaria.

The Yellowhammer

Bwlch y Cariad

Type	Unclassified
Grid Reference	SS 84089 77236
Parish	Newton Nottage
County	Glamorgan
When recorded	1898–1908
Primary Source	OS 2nd Edition Maps
Secondary Source	Great Britain 1900 website
Notes	Imported from GB1900

He guessed where the girl had gone.

She'd gone to the watching place.

That's where the girl had gone.

They'd been there together once only, but Ffrez remembered everything. Clever, wasn't she? That's what everybody used to say. But now being clever wasn't enough.

She'd know the path. A trace, that's all it had been. A line in the sand. If it was still there, which he knew it couldn't be. Yet, she'd find her way. Up to that stone. It was a white stone, an exposed part of the limestone ridge. But when he had examined it himself the colour was created by lichen. Countless tiny white hairs.

He remembered he had made his way up the dune through old bracken and new fern. Then edged under the hawthorn that shrouded the outcrop. He'd found he could sit there unseen. A perfect place to watch. To observe the slopes and the sea.

Cai had asked himself what other people might have sat where he did, completely concealed, under the may tree. Chewing hawthorn leaves some called bread and cheese. Thoughtful. Or at ease. No reason to hide.

Yes, children would have hidden. Under an earlier tree. A maytree thousands of years ago. A boy, a man, looking out as he did, as the waves came in. Were they good sets? Why didn't people surf in those days, those Bronze Age, those prehistoric days? The days when the bluestones passed on the rafts. The days before the sand blew in. The days before the hurricanes…

No, it wasn't difficult to imagine other people. Because to sit on the white stone was a statement. Of ownership. He supposed whoever sat there in the past wanted to be seen. But now concealment was everything.

He remembered the clefts in the stone. Narrow enough to hide a CD. Yes, he could remember those. And a simcard

easily. A whole life's work on a chip, no bigger than a hawthorn petal. These days everyone wanted to tell their story.
Because everyone had a story to tell. Ffrez especially, with
her own music, repeating, repeating her chords. Christ, she
was driving him spare, all hours, all hours... But Cai supposed it was natural. She was recording her music, he was
helping, different versions over and over. Why couldn't she
ever get it right? Why...

Yeah, the girl had gone to Gorwelion. That very minute she might be looking down at the sea. Higher than the
white stone, hidden in the fern and the firetrees. From
there she would see the floods and the ruined fairground,
a whole new coastline, and now the lakes between the
dunes. Those smashed dunes like islands. Some of them
had names, didn't they? Like tiny countries. In the eve-
nings the sand on their shoulders was indigo...

Once, he'd found a message in a bottle on the beach,
released from not far away. A child's round handwriting
dated after one of the storms. Cai had kept it and was
meaning to...what? Throw his own bottle in the surf? He
remembered taking the duct tape off the plastic jar, unroll-
ing the letter. Wondering, amazed.... A letter in a bottle? A
real one. Didn't get far, did it?

And look at these, he thought, these pages, torn from notebooks and ringbinders, the pages Ffrez was trying to collate, the papers the others had trodden over until she had
screamed out. She'd told them they were asking to stay

DELIRIUM

stupid forever. Because these were the pages the old man
had written in his diaries. That they were standing upon.
Or using as toilet paper. Boy, she'd gone mad that morning.
Never seen her like that before. He wrote those pages, she
shouted. And you're wiping your shitty arse with his life...

But the old man's writing was so difficult to understand.
It was his own private language. Who had time for such
things, any more? Who had time...?

But Ffrez was scanning the pages. Making up for..?
She was digitalizing what she called the archive, half way
through the notebooks, every word, even the incompre-
hensible ramblings, even the lies. Because who could tell?
Didn't mean the old man told the truth, did it? Because it
was written down? Look, just another fairground dreamer,
wasn't he? Drinking in that pub that was flooded out. And
now here's Ffrez saying pick up the pages. Could be a mas-
terpiece, she said. Might show the way out of all this...

Christ, Cai thought. Fat chance. Just mutterings of the
old man's madness. Now about to be preserved on a chip.
Forever. As if it was important. As if someone might learn
from all of that useless boasting...

That day on the stone he'd looked out at the slack, over to
the swell and the sets coming in, the waves good, the finials
smoking. And he'd seen it change, the weather in a minute,
the weather warp... He'd told them all, the old man, mam,
Slobo. Ffrez was off somewhere on her own...

Because he'd described the twister that came over the
sea. Cold on his skin, it was, and the birds silent, only those

birds crying that were trapped in the storm's *twndish*, that were flung out of the whirlwind as it whipped over the dune. Pitiful sound, he'd always thought, gazing himself into the tornado's black wires, sand in his hair.

Yeah, well…. Now he looked at the girl's shelves in the barn. Okay, he had promised not to. Okay, sworn never to, but if she would trail out alone…. Even if she came back and found him nosing, there was no problem. Shouldn't be precious, should she?

But yes, thought Cai, she's meticulous. Everything alphabetical, her music, her books. Look at this: JS Bach piano, JS Bach harpsichord, JS Bach three piano Goldberg Variations, two harpsichord Goldberg variations, JS Bach cello, JS Bach choral, JS Bach the partitas, JS Bach orchestral…. Tons of it. Then, ha ha, Beastie Boys…. She was even doing it to the old man's diaries, imposing her system. Which he would have hated. That sense of order of hers? A place for everything and everything in..? Not now, hardly. Every system was smashed. Floated away…. But maybe it's the only way to build again.

Bloody Ffrez had method, he had to agree. She collected corals. She filed fossils. Here they were, each with its names. That's why she'd gone to Gorwelion. To see what the latest storm had uncovered. Because that was the sand's lesson, they both agreed. What the sand concealed was not always what the sand revealed.

He switched on the player. Yeah, this was her latest craze. Those Babylonian songs she had discovered. Or, that were given by one of her girlfriends. Those feminists weeing themselves about another dead language. Or, a made up language. Was that worse? Because nobody really knew how the music should sound. The people playing it were interpreting ideas from old texts. And the singer? American. Typical.

He looked at the barn. Big and draughty, patches of mould. They'd insulated as best they could. Bubblewrap, carpet, all those sacks of vermiculite, even some of the old man's papers he'd used when Ffrez wasn't looking. She said it had to be like one of those Japanese hotels, divided up like a honeycomb. All those tiny rooms that people rented! So the barn was now ten cells, the tractor, immoveable, still parked where it had always been. Ffrez would sit there, against the huge tyre, headphones on, or plinking chords.

What's an ominous chord? she'd asked everyone.

Find one in good old JS, Cai had said. And she settled to her work again...

He listened to the singer. The girl was working out the words of those dead songs. Those never-been songs. Singing in a language she'd never heard, spoken or sung. Like that yellowhammer going round in the whirlwind. Yeah, pitiful....

And I saw that bird, he thought. It fell at my feet. I could hardly stand up that afternoon. Its neck was broken, I saw. And now you never see them. You never see or hear them. But how could a storm do that..?

Then Ffrez had said a strange thing. She said those birds sometimes gave a newborn chick to the adders. So the snakes wouldn't eat the other chicks. Kind of a sacrifice.

No, he'd said. Don't be daft. What bird would do that? But yes, they lived together, she said. In the dunes under the gorse. Yellow as gorse petals, those birds…. The diamonds on the snakes black and yellow.

He remembered school, the way the drawers in the cabinets were marked with a handwritten slip of paper, the specimen jars the same. And the writing faded as if it was ancient. Like something pulled out of the dune. He'd been in the laboratory once alone. How it all seemed to smell, he noticed, the formaldehyde worse than damp in the barn.

But, fair play, the music was good. Babylonian tears, he thought. Does Ffrez shed those? Does it make her cry when she's on her own? Because she can cry, she can cry. How often have I see it? But if only she could come up with something like that Babylon song herself…. Something catchy. Forget ominous. Because ominous is everywhere… Just a simple backbeat. He could do that, yes. And mix her voice low, so the words were mysterious… Words without meaning because the sound was everything, he agreed with her there.

Cai switched on the music again. Ffrez's note described the song as 'The Flood'. Well, she'd discover exactly what their own situation was like now. The sea could enter the dunes after the last blow out…. Seawater mixing with fresh. What would that mean?

He thought about their latest joint expedition. Dovydas, who had one of the honeycomb rooms in the barn, had come too. They'd walked up to the quarry, the three of them quarrelling for some reason, so they didn't get there till late. Not dusk, they wouldn't have attempted it, but the stupid disagreement had slowed them down. Ffrez could be so insistent that it drove him mad. She wasn't always right, was she? Dovydas agreed with him, but no, he didn't have the guts to stand up against Ffrez. None of the others did.

The lagoon had startled Cai. It always did. Turquoise, Dovydas said, who had never seen it before, and was rarely descriptive.

Blue, Cai had insisted. Because what would a Lithuanian know?

But he was right, Cai supposed. The quarry was an enormous limestone bowl created by blasting. Various streams ran into it and there must have been a way out for the water too, because its level never seemed to get higher…. Cai had looked at the lagoon and thought something was wrong with it. But it had been Ffresni who described the pollution in it, the reasons for that chemical blue….

The three of them had stood behind the waterfall that poured into the lake. Behind this stretched the cave they decided to enter. There was evidence of other visitors, but it seemed none had been recent. Clothes, sticks, sweet wrappings were scattered around. Ffrez had led the way.

Quiet now, she'd hissed.

We know, Cai had spat back.

Look at this, the girl had said to Dovydas. What you think this is? In this rock

Ahead was a stone table. It had been cut by hand out of the cave itself and resembled an altar. Ffrez stepped up.

You won't know what to look for, Ffrez had said. She shone her torch over the table, revealing faint lines. Then Cai had pushed forward.

Fossil, he said. Looks like a fish, doesn't it? You can see where the bones were. They were blasting rock out of the quarry and they found this thing. Brought it in here for safekeeping. Soon after that everything became too... difficult. So it's stuck here...

A fish? whispered Dovydas. Cai noted they were all three whispering.

They found themselves on the cliff above the lagoon, the sky snowlit, thunderlit, the colour of snow and thunder being violet, almost ultraviolet, Ffresni had said of that violent light.

Well, she would have said that, Cai had sneered to himself. Wrong. As usual. That's her wanting the last word...

The three stood together and watched volleys of hailstones prick the water. At their heaviest the lagoon looked as if something had been disturbed in its depths. But it was Ffrez who spoke for them all.

There's nothing there. No fish, no eels. Fish might be brought in by the streams but can't live in that. It's the calcite that turns it blue...

We used to swim in it, Cai had added to Dovydas. Just didn't put our heads under...

But maybe we could live here, suggested Dovydas. The waterfall hides the cave. Like a curtain, don't you think? I mean, for a while...

It's good where we are, Ffrez had said immediately.

Again, you see. Making our decisions for us. As usual.

Ffrez & Taran: The Satyr

For me he'll always be the old man. I found this in one of
those Moleskine notebooks, part of that hoard he left. That
almighty mess. We knew he was writing everything down
but this is with dates and locations, as if he thought someone might read it. Or care about that indecipherable life he
led.

You've seen some of his archive but new things keep
turning up in unexpected places. Loose pages ripped
from exercise books, scrawls on the backs of other people's letters. Some of you boys wiped your shitty arses
with those pages and I'm still angry about that. But you
know the stuff, how he arrived in Albania or got on a bus
from Baghdad. Yes, why couldn't he have written a blog
like everybody else?

Yet maybe his life is all too clear. Seems his condition
was worse than we thought. Periods of delirium when the
malaria came back, not to mention that incident he boasted

about. This has a title too, 'The Satyr', and here's what I
copied from the Moleskine. Honest, word for word.

The Satyr

*They were in a favoured spot a few miles off the Tunisian coast.
When they pulled up the net there was a leg in it. Along with the
sardines and the anchovies there was a statue's leg.*

*On every expedition afterwards they thought maybe this time
we'll get the whole body. And you know? They did. A year later
this green creature was hauled over the side. The leg belonged to
the body and the body to the leg. The crew of the Fat Captain out
of western Sicily had been proved right. But that's the Tunisian
coast for you. Hidden wonders, and that statue as Greek as it gets.*

*The five of us had felt like swifts, rising. That town was full
of swifts but even when we reached the top and looked around
we still didn't know where the voice was coming from. Until
someone glanced up. And there she was, a young woman, beck-
oning.*

*Woo hoo! Here, here! she was calling. So we climbed three
flights and she said, please, come and look at this. I show all
passing visitors.*

*This woman took us outside on to a balcony and we crowded
in. The ones at the back couldn't understand but those in front
realised straightaway what she wanted us to see.*

*It was the view. The frightening panorama from that apart-
ment. The town is at a difficult altitude already but those
buildings, tall themselves, had been constructed on the very*

81

summit. Only one of the churches stood above it. And so we looked straight out toward Etna.

Giddying, I tell you. Made me sick, it was so sudden. That was the top of the world and we were gazing across slopes of black lava at smoke from the volcano and that cloud that always seems to hang there. A double warning, I thought, that smoke, that cloud. But everyone seemed to take it as normal. Just like history, they ignored the dangers.

I think she was Romanian. Gave us all an almond biscuit, a thimble of coffee, and said in English, so what do you think?

Marvellous, we said. Because she was clearly proud. This was her apartment and she was entertaining spur of the moment guests. Her spur, her moment. She said every morning she and her daughter ate breakfast on that balcony.

I had to step away. Even when I braved a second look I needed to grasp the rail. The world I knew had vanished so there was nothing under my feet. Maybe it's a sign of ageing but everything started to swim around me.

Later in the square people asked us where we were staying. We waited for one another to speak before it dawned that we didn't know the house's name.

With Beppe, we said. That's where. You must know Beppe. But everyone we met in that square seemed to be called Beppe. It was St. Anthony's Day and the women were preparing a feast. The men were already outside, the old men in the square at their tables, men who looked like they had been sitting there for a thousand years.

Working in the square was a child. Ned, they called him, but I'm not sure if that was his name. He talked to us in English but said he spoke three languages, Italian, French, Arabic, and we believed him. So maybe that's four. When you're mono like I am it gets embarrassing. Too late now I thought, I'm plain stupid. Another form of vertigo.

This diary tells me exactly a year ago I became acquainted with the landscape of my own brain. Those photographs of a CT scan could have been a black walnut. My consultant pointed out two white patches, tracing them with a biro. He called them lesions.

How's the memory? he asked.

I had to think before I answered.

Fine, I replied. And stared him down. Christ, even in that conversation I was trying to bluff. As if he hadn't been holding all the cards...

Look, he said, you're of a certain age. Anyone scanned is going to show something. I know I would. But these indicate damage and each lesion is the evidence.

To me the scars looked like radioactive burns. Something uranium might leave on the skin, so powerful it had seared straight in. But that's a death sentence...

Okay, I'm also starting now to think I'm prone to dizziness. On one of our days at the house I fell asleep and Beppe joked about the heat, saying I wasn't used to it.

Which is true. Anyway, that first day we were late. It had been difficult to reach the house as there were collapsed roads among those hills. It's earthquake country, remember.

All we could hear in the silence were goat bells. I'd glance up from my table under the willow and think, there's nothing here to stop me getting on with…what? Finding the right word? I don't think that would have impressed Ned. But I'd ensured I could write from a table outside. The perfect place for a desk.

Okay, I nodded off and suddenly there was Venus looking over one shoulder and Jupiter over the other. Where had the day gone? Where had all the days gone?

Yes, Beppe's house was like a dream but I swear everything I'm writing down actually happened. On that land is a well with a wooden cover for that well and a bucket on a pulley and the wellwater a long way down like light at a tunnel's end.

To tell the truth I hated travelling through those Italian tunnels when I first drove there and back in the lorry. Subterranean homesick, that was me, sweaty palms on the steering wheel of a big white Iveco.

But somehow we were in the Iveco together, me, Beppe, Ned, the Romanian, all of us. Susan from Palermo was there too, complaining about the marble staircases of another palazzo, taking the bags upstairs, downstairs on those impossible steps. She told us she was born in Kenya and her daughter in Italy. But the girl wanted to speak English. So Susan asked us straight out, could they both come over to..? Did we think..? Was there a chance..?

Took us all by surprise but it's the inevitable question. Why not? we all barked. Of course, I could have told her why not but didn't have the heart. I was too ashamed.

Yes, the bottom of the well or light in the tunnel. And in the distance were the temples at Agrigento. They must be what some of the migrants see when they come north in those boats. There in the mist before dawn are pillars above the beach. Temples that have stood for nearly three thousand years. The first sign of Europe for those travellers.

The best of us, I'd say, those people. Transfixed by the myth of our world of push button tides and digital air con. By our anti-histamine ecology.

But how quickly 'migrant' has become a dirty word. They were gambling everything, trying the old routes, forging new ones. What do we expect? Their phones show them the bounty that might be won. And it's us on those phones. We're making the calls. I promise you those people are coming all the way. We can't stop life.

I blame the sun and another glass of Grillo. Yes, I woke under the willow. Such was breakfast, a blood orange, the chilly white. But don't think I've not seen the malarial babies and the old people with glaucoma. Seen the desperate and the brilliant who brought them. They had been hidden in the backs of Ivecos, then were afloat for days, padlocked into holds. Galleyslaves, I tell you, all their money spent on broken down guzzos, on inflatables or any Libyan ketch half trustworthy. Trafficked.

Which is exactly the right word. Like drugs, but we need those drugs. I might have done it myself, driving the lorry back that time from Durazzo, a family hidden in its sleeping compartment. Only I went under the Alps, while they're coming across the Med…

It was me smuggled the child across the Sham desert in that bus out of Baghdad. Or was it our camera, swaddled to protect it from dust? It might easily have been a baby. That Sony trav-elled on my lap for twenty-four hours and there I sat, smoothing its brow, checking its pulse, staring out at the worst landscape you could imagine. As if the moon was black.

I'd seen our cameraman, doing the same, stroking the Sony and calling it 'my daughter, my daughter...' We'd met his real daughter, aged twelve, standing up in her cot, humming a lullaby. Palsied, the poor kid. When I looked into her eyes I thought I was swimming. Bottomless, those pools...

Yes, I felt giddy. It was Beppe's voice that woke me. But I remember the dream he interrupted. You see, there's a story for everyone. Only we've stopped listening. We can't take it any more. But do you know what it means if you stop listening?

We all warmed to Beppe because he loved that land. It was his family's immemorial land and his grandmother lives there still. But Beppe talked about his home like a man who's returned from a bad place.

So, he cooked for us and told us about the different ricotta, and the pigs he fed on fennel. He promised we would taste the aniseed in his pork. It was that meat he prepared outside after I found enough firewood. It was his own olive oil too and his fennel in the orange salad. All that fennel, that's why the fields were yellow. Those people simply cooked what they grew.

Reading between the lines, Beppe had covered the water-front. The actual word he used was 'playboy', but I don't think he knew what that implied. So I'm trying to translate. He was speaking English but he tried to explain his own lan-guage to us.

We were out in the dusk one night, counting the constellations, a blizzard of moths in the mosquito lamps as we talked. Around here we don't see moths anymore. It's taken me years to notice what's missing now. Which means it's too late...

Anyway, there are two planets together, he told us. For this special occasion. Yes, it's rare, we said. Coming together like that. I didn't ask him which was which. So now I know the central upper Sicilian for 'stars'. Or, I know the sound my mouth should make when I say that word. Kind of humbling. Maybe that's why I was lying down, trying to find the right music for the word. Or perhaps I was looking at the sky.

Yes, where had all those days gone? At dusk on the last day it was time to light the fire. Beppe was a busy man but when he texted he would be coming home with his own food I found myself nominated to gather firewood. Position of honour, so I listed everything I could find: olive, aloe, prickly pear, kindled with cactus our firelight on the hill. Sicilian driftwood in the air and snow on Etna still.

Thinking about that town, little Ned ruled the square, serving granita, juggling plates. He even had time to play football with us but it can be hard to get your ball back in that place. Boy, he was being run ragged but always kept a smile on his face. As if he was delighted to be alive. And around him sat the old men in their appointed places, tiny vermilion drinks set before them. Drinks they never touched.

Guess who Ned reminded me of? After it was put together I looked at the statue in a museum in Mazara. Beautiful child, I thought. Sea-faun with bronze braids over a Syrian face. Elf

*ears too, unmistakable. It was supposed to be a satyr, dancing in
bliss. The sculptor had captured the creature in a two thousand
year old casting. Being a satyr, there's a considerable Luigi.
Fair enough, I thought. And satyrs were not circumcised. But a
gorgeous sea-beast, that dancer in a dusty room. Mafioso with
alabaster eyes.*

*After that last meal he cooked for us on the open fire our time
was up. We had to leave and I realized we wouldn't be seeing
Beppe again. But what he did was to spell out the name of the
house where we'd been staying. That house we couldn't explain.
'San Todaro' I think his writing says.*

*Above all Beppe was careful to show us the white stone where
we should hide the key to the gates when we left for the final
time. A stone amongst other stones in the fennel field.*

*And that's the last thing Beppe said to us. When we leave
San Todaro, climbing its broken road, to be sure the gates beside
the well and the willow are locked. It's the only way to stay
safe."*

That's it. That's how 'The Satyr' reads, spread over
twenty-three Moleskine pages.

But what did some people call the old man? Taran, that was
it. The god of thunder, a god who could make children cry
and grown men duck their heads. Yes, a not inconsiderable
god. Forgotten I suppose? As they all must be. But, I tell you,
there's more to come. And we have to save what's left.

Cai: The Yellowhammer

He looked at himself in the sliver of mirror, saw grey bristles on the left cheek.

Just like the old man, he realised, the colour of the old bastard's beard when he refused to shave. The same place, under the left ear. Oddly luxuriant there. Christ, he was becoming his father. Same eyebrows too.

But he could still see her face. And he was shocked by the whole experience. The girl's expression when she turned was terrified. Young, maybe sixteen, and out in the woods. What was she doing there? Seemed to be making her way back to some camp, or maybe coming away from that camp, as if ordered to go foraging for food. For anything.

No more than sixteen, and skinny. No, fourteen. All right, she could have been twelve. A girl alone in that place, a fallen ashtree and reefs of bluebells stretching into the shade. Blue into dark blue into darkness. Perhaps the colour of the Messina Straits the old man had talked about.

Sometimes *indigo* had been his word. What was certain it was somewhere Cai would never visit.

He had felt a jolt in his chest. Christ, he'd farted in surprise, a crack in the guts, outrage in his arsehole, so unexpected was their meeting. The last thing he'd been expecting.... Okay, dreaming again, wasn't he. He'd switched off for just a second. Well, there was no law against that.

The couple had almost collided. Yet Cai had had no indication she was there. And the girl likewise, the blue eyed-child, appalled at his step towards her in that place. That place of all places. How could he have seen her in her vest, that girl in green disguise, brownskinned kid, and her throat's pale slash only inches away as she spun round to accuse him... A thin black bra strap down her shoulder not concealed by the camouflage.

She had appeared fully formed out of the trees. Toxic nymph, weren't they all? But who'd be a girl?

Okay, in that place there were walls buried in moss, as if there had been houses once, but no buildings were marked on old or recent maps. A farm maybe, before the trees had come out of the sand, before the sand itself had blown. The dunes will never stay the same, the old man had warned. You can't trust sand.

Cai had been meaning to explore but there was too much to do. His father had never talked about this valley, and neither had Ffrez mentioned it. Just a nameless cleft between sandhills. But steep, yes steep...

No, he couldn't remember being there before. At least, not that path. But maybe the girl wouldn't have known either. Because he was taking care, taking care as he always did. Not surprising he might startle her. They were scavengers, after all. They'd learned bushcraft of a sort. But he couldn't forget her. And now he never would...

Amongst what he'd kept was a plastic bag of one thousand disposable razors. These were orange Bics, serviceable for initial use, soon dull. There must have been hundreds of razors still in the bag, found in the house they had occupied, the house with the helicopter pad. They'd been there not long previously. The house was being built at the same time as Beach Road was in the process of abandonment, despite the limestone boulders lorried out to bolster the defences.

Was it Katia had shrugged the first boulders aside? Or The Beast? It didn't matter now, that was a question for history. For those who come after. But suddenly shaving, this morning, 5a.m. and the light a benediction, appealed. Because he needed to be clean.

For Cai, shaving was once a week since he rid himself of the beard. Not that he had ever managed full growth. *Straggly* was the word people used. Yeah, Sparkle and especially Ffrez, said he looked straggly. Son of his father, wasn't he? The old man had tried to start a beard, but mam had turned the pressure up, saying he looked unwashed. Jesus.

Once at best? Okay, every fortnight. But now in this light...it demanded.

So why today? Who cared? Get rid of the week's stubble. A clean start. Even with cold water, which wasn't so good. Cai remembered hot water, the bathroom full of steam and the scummy line of shaved hair. Tide on the slipway. What it left behind. Hairs in the plughole. Because nothing stays a secret long...

And once, yes, Cai had used the old man's cologne, felt its thrilling sting. That gold bottle, what was it called? Looked expensive, too. Just a splash? Another of the old man's little foibles. Said he inherited it, and no, of course he hadn't actually paid money for it. Did they think he was that stupid? As if...

But wine or food, the old man prided himself. That gin he bought for Mam, now. *Portobello Road*, that was something special, even she agreed. Yes, *Portobello Road* gin. As to the cologne, only a dab, the old man had always said, even towards the end. When they were shaving him themselves. Those last drops they'd tried to squeeze from the gold bottle. Yes, Christian, Clive Christian, and the bottle long dry. Not even a dab remaining. No Christian dregs...

But yes he wanted to feel cleaner than he'd ever been. All those Bics the French had made? The fucking Chinese? What had Bic done? Sponsored the *Tour de France*, the old man had said once, and Cai could hear his voice as he now selected a razor and started scraping the stubble, a soap and coldwater shave, the old man's voice in his head.

He'd always claimed to be a ventriloquist, hadn't he, the bastard? And so many dummies, he'd had, mam and Ffrez and yes, himself. All his life a dummy.

Cai shaved under his ears as best he could, pulled at his nostrils, stretched his cheeks. Suddenly his own blood was on the floor. First droplet, then a second. Fat and hot like thunderstorm rain. The new thunder.

More than a dab, he thought. But those walls, he'd never noticed them before. Fallen stones under a quilt of moss. And no, neither of them made a sound, did they? The leaves now flat and the flowers' white bulbs come right out of the sand. As if people had been dancing there...

Taran: The Palestinian

The white arse?

Three words on a piece of paper. That's what the old man called the bird. So I did too. The only time I saw it was in the Gwter Gryn with cliffs on three sides. Not a good place for the tide to catch you.

They're here from April, those white arses. Till they go back to wherever they come from. Grey with that white flash. Close up there's a line on the face like a lightning bolt. Kind of David Bowie cosmetic stripe, the old man said. Made it unmistakable, he thought.

I can't remember the bird's real name. I can't remember David Bowie. But that's what the old man called it.

*

That's a sheet torn from a diary, said Ffrez. April 20th, and his scrawl in pencil. On its own so far, without context.

These pages show he wrote constantly about the Gwter Gryn. He was always a beachcomber.

The woman had gathered all the material she could carry, notebooks and magazines. Some of it was dated yet might be unintelligible. It would be a life's work going through those boxes. She had put plastic sheeting over the bale of manuscripts, reading fragments in the evening. But more papers kept turning up.

Most important to her were the old man's letters. Those to her personally she'd added to the hoard. All his correspondence from Festival Island she kept in a plastic wallet.

By doing this she suspected she was joining a game long organized. Was she becoming the old man's archivist? She felt resentful but picked out the first letter.

Dear Ffrez

It was your mother insisted on Ffresni. She was working as a nursing assistant in one of the care homes. There was a sign on a door, 'Ffresni's Room', and she commented on the name. Better than Freshness, she thought. So from way back it was a name your mother wanted. That's how it goes, kid. You end up living someone else's idea…

No, don't blame my mother, she said to herself. You planned all this.

After skipping a few lines she continued reading:

Took an Abu Dhabi flight. Seven hours, first elated then numbed by gin. Sour Etihad stuff but worked fine. Not a trace of the old problem. Noted there was a library in the terminal so left some books in Arabic translation. I know, I know, but that's what people like me do. Self-publicists till we die. Then the helicopter arrived and the two of us waiting were taken away…. No, we didn't speak, we were well past that.

But I wanted the view. The desert below was the colour of a buzzard's breast…. Kind of frothy coffee. Bird I never liked, by the way. Think I understand why the crows always gang up. Then, a red sun in the Empty Quarter.

And finally the ocean. In the evening light it was indigo. No other word allowed. Some white fringes where the waves broke. I asked the pilot how many islands in the Gulf and he said they're not sure. New islands are being made as we speak. Volcanic activity.

'It's unstable round here' he said.

I liked that. More than wry.

Then he pointed out Yas Island which holds Ferrari World. Yes, I drove fast as a young man but most of the writers I know never learned. I think their brains are wired differently. As I get older the more dubious about speed I've become. Ferraris leave me cold. Next door was Warner Brothers. I didn't even glance.

But the last word the pilot spoke was 'there'. When we looked we saw what we'd been promised, 'a dhow-shaped island in a solar sea'. Some marketing type had written that but I was hooked. And green too, our island. Some of the rarest palms transplanted, including those that died out in Baghdad after the Gulf Wars and UN sanctions.

We landed in a compound. I counted three drones and a fleet of Mercedes 4x4s. The island is all dunes and beaches. Remind you of anywhere? But the house is astonishing. They've spelled my name wrong on my stationery, but it's in gold, so fair enough. Bowls of fruit, Portobello gin. Yes, they've done their homework on me. But a quote from Manley Hopkins in a biodegradable tube?... "In the life I lead now, which is one of a continually jaded and harassed mind, if in any leisure I try to do anything I make no way...." *What the..? There'll be another tube very soon...*

'Festival Island' we call it. Can't remember its real name. (I know how you love irony, Ffrez.) The only inhabitants had been pearl fishers. Maybe a few remain...

It might be someone's idea of paradise. A real desert island. But the emir who inherited it had once been to the Hay and Toronto Harbourfront festivals, and with oil money he can do anything he wishes. So, Festival Island has become a big ticket invitation.

You've never been on a writing course, Ffrez, but it's along those lines. Science and peace Nobel laureates. An Albanian poet like Trotsky in a Steffano Ricci tie. Then talkshow philosophers from the States, maharishi economists. With their PAs and personal chefs, their pissed off children and English rose nannies. A festival that lasts six months...

And the punters? Some will park their yachts in Qatar, buying into the next big thing. Namely this. They don't believe they can get it in Marbella.

But why are they here? To breathe the same air as all us geniuses. I kid you not, kiddo. And why me? Friend of a friend's recommendation. Sick joke, maybe. Anyway, I'm one of several writers-in-rez, so I've promised to hand over every gorgeous sentence. But I'm writing about another world. The past. Because I'll always be old school. I'll never catch up with myself.

The girl scowled and turned a page.

The emir even has his own currency. The 'solar dirham' is how we're paid.... No, I haven't met him yet. Maybe he doesn't exist. Pictures are of a tall man with a hawk's nose. Appropriate. These people, how they quarter the world!

The only person I've spoken to is the transport co-ordinator, Omar Abudeeb. Stepped out of the darkness last night from behind my mashrabiya wall. I was on my patio, sitting with coffee. A woman in black had brought it. All I have to do is nod and more coffee arrives. Sweetmeats too. That's my latest favourite word. Next, I'll try the cocktails. Just another nod. All beck no call.

Already I'm used to Omar's cigarettes. I know nobody's allowed to smoke here, which is strict for the Gulf, but he ignores the rule. I like that.

Maybe one hundred a day, he said when I asked him.

Don't believe you, I said.

One hundred and ten sometimes, he repeated. And wrote it on the air.

It'll kill you, I said.

I am Palestinian, he said. Should I care?

In the twilight I couldn't tell if he was smiling.

You have a job.

Oh yes.

You speak English…

But not like you.

He might have smiled then. My children are not here, he said. They never can be….

In the dark I could see only the cigarette's glow, the shape of his face. His eyes were invisible but I recalled how they looked in their hollows. Colour of smoke. Hunted, maybe. No, haunted. The other worker I've spoken to is a Ukrainian behind the bar. Yes, bar. Rules are fluid here, it seems. He spoke English too and I imagine his Arabic is non-existent. Part of the tide, Freshness. As are all of us.

Don't ask how these people arrived on the island. I've stopped trying to make sense of it. Survival of the fittest, kid, or the luckiest, and here's me pretending I have something new to say. And I'll go on pretending till the contract is up…

But solar dirhams, Ffrez! The new currency of sunlight. Getting paid this way feels… honourable. The money is some-how clean. Last evening I watched the solar panels make their last adjustment before nightfall. Black sunflowers counting the steps of the sun…

{*Later*}.

It's morning now. I've been sitting and wondering what I'm really doing. In my garden (yes!) the heat feels like cast iron over my head, but indoors is the drench of aircon. The coffee might not come with cardamom as it did in Baghdad but just one gesture and the woman who hovers like a hummingbird will appear from somewhere…. But all in black. Impossibly modest…

Omar says the women's salons are the best gigs. My first is due in three weeks so no pressure. An interview and reading of the work I begin here. Surely not a big audience. But it's women who feed this culture. Who keep it going with their curiosity. Oil in its barrels, gas in cubic whatever and an obscene amount of money have made the world dull, Ffrez. That's why the emira is ambitious for her island. Maybe it's her mistake I'm here…

I'm looking at her programme now. Zero carbon house building, farming on Mars. The landscape I saw yesterday looked pretty martian. It seemed to spell out the atrocity of thirst. Worthy stuff, yes, but too late for me. Oh, and a talk titled "The Promise of Cryonics". There will be someone explaining how she can freeze memory…

Better start with me, then. I can't recall yesterday without my notebook. But no need for Omar yet. He's obsessed with his children. Hasn't seen them for a year. I pointed out those children don't exist any more. That they're different people now. I don't think he understood me, which is just as well.

But he's so thin. Skin the colour of olive oil. White shirt, grey slacks but that yellow tinge to him.

I think today counts as my second morning, Ffrez. So another tube has arrived. This one holds a translation: "The world has not enough to satisfy ambition." Then a last line: "Shame won't win the smallest thing."

Fifteen hundred years old, Ffrez, this poem. I wonder if the emir chooses the quotes himself. Or the emira? Maybe it's done by algorithm? I'm beginning to think they're all personalised. After all, they knew about the gin. So I'm, trying to work out what they say about me and what tomorrow's tube will bring.

Record heat here once again, apparently. I thought my highest was 125 F. But this island beats everything. Perhaps it's the world's first heliocracy…

Ffresni turned another page. At last she'd grown used to the handwriting.

I'd asked Omar to come back when he had time. Got a whiff of those Hollywood Premiums before I saw him. And he looked even thinner to me. Sweat in his armpits. My diminutive Shadrach, smelling of the fire…

Okay, he's missing his children. But I'm missing all of you. I told him I once stood on the Golan Heights and the borders were explained to me. Impossibly complicated. But growing on the hillsides were olive trees. Twisted like Hebrew characters or awkward as the Arabic alphabet. Languages I can't read. But I eat the olives.

She turned a page.

So you've been there? asked Omar.
A mirror smashed by a tank track, I said. That's Palestine. Yeah, I've been.

Omar blew smoke.

Well...? he asked.

Look, I said, where I come from there are black plastic bags hanging in the bushes. Bags full of dogshit. Would you rather your dogshit on the ground or hanging in the trees?

Omar laughed at that.

You know what those bags remind me of? I asked. Something I saw in your Palestine.

What?

Pears, I'd thought at first. Hard little pears. Green pears hanging in the trees. But bomblets. Yes, strange word, that. Sounds like something gentle. Something that swings over a cradle. But full of seeds, those pears. Go straight through you. Hard little pears. Hanging in the trees of Palestine...

How typical of the old man, she thought, putting down the page. One thing reminding him of another. They never knew what he was thinking. Flakey or what?

*

Yes, a white arse in the Gwter Gryn. But he couldn't swim, you know. I suppose he was afraid of the water, mangy old lion, though what bothered us was the riptide in his blood.

But the best thing, Ffrez, he used to say, is sand.

Once in the Gwter he told us the sand there felt like hot silk. I remember him saying, "when people examine the grains they're white and purple and... nothing like sand at all...."

And I wonder whether migrants will ever wash up here. Anything's possible now. But limestone's like razorblades in the Gwter, it would rip a dinghy to shreds. Even if there are coldwater pearls.

Don't think he ever filmed there. But who knows what's in the boxes...? And at least he had the chance to leave something behind...

(1) Whitearse – wheatear, tinwen y graig
(2) From a letter by Gerard Manley Hopkins to Robert Bridges, 1.9.1885.
(3) Lines taken from Gwyn Thomas's translation of 'Gorchan Maeldderw' in *Gododdin: The Earliest British Literature* (Gomer, 2012). Attributable to Taliesin.

Ffrez: Marooned

1.

Not long before, they'd found someone in a blue Rab Neutrino sleeping bag. Nobody wanted to take the body out. She thought she should but it was impossible...

Ach! she hissed. The grave's banquet. She remembered a dead sheep on the beach. But when she approached she noticed it was breathing. After a while she realized its corpse was full of crabs.

In the end they dug a pit for the dead boy. He was wearing a mask but she zipped him almost all the way up. Till the teeth snagged...

2.

Cuttlebone?
Goatwillowstick?
Jay's feather in a purse?

If the dogs didn't scatter her bones, what might she leave? Because she could split as easily as birch bark, that was clear. Wide in the white wood her black wounds opening.

So there she is: steelies scuffed raw and Czech army surplus olive green thermal socks. But that sound?

A footstep in the sand?

Or water against the sand?

Or sand against shattered glass?

Yes, something to do with sand. Surely.

Full moon over the crest. A super-moon they called it once. Two of the four turbines were visible from there, two miles away…. Another angle would reveal all four, one with a broken blade, covered in bracken and willow. Sheared and fallen in one of the hurricanes last year…. The year before?

3.

She tries the night goggles again. No, nothing there. Or here. But… flies? Dust in the air? No, flies. Tiny…. Everywhere…. But no fires that she can see on the dunes. Doesn't mean….

From darkness she looks at the lake. There are waves upon it, moving west to east and yes, if she listens she can hear the water lapping. She comes through the willow down the side of the dune. Pre-dawn, nothing but the water, almost inaudible.

Five o'clock, she guesses. Not that it matters. But 5 am in November. The black month as people used to call it. Now she wonders how she might ever feel more alert. It's good to be scared. Isn't it?

Never more alive than…. Christ, she thinks, looking at the surface of the dune slack and the moonlight running through it. Higher than she could ever remember.

She raises her eyes in the night goggles. Yes, she's correct, on the other side a deer has come down to the edge. A black deer. Behind it, a fawn. Both deer pause to drink, cautious in the green light created by Nightvision. Supernatural this colour, she has always thought.

It looks black, that hind. Therefore a roe deer, she decides. Big for the dunes and unexpected. Might have swum the river with the younker. Displaced by the storm. But harassed by dogs, probably. So many dogs these days. Feral, starving…

She remembers the old man's diaries, some looseleaf pages scattered on the barn floor. *Skanderbeg* was underlined twice, and *5.10am. Dogs. Moonlight on the square. Where the hell are the people? Where…? So many dogs…*

Same time now.

As best she could she had tidied the pages. Maybe her own grey footprints upon them. He'd seen everything, the old man. That's what he claimed. Well, he never saw anything like this. Silly old…

The last time she recalled seeing him he'd bought ice cream in the fairground. Yes, Billionaires' shortbread. That's what she'd chosen from fifty flavours at Bardi's…

But she's surprised there is no dog sound now, as she crouches lower in the willows. The leaves are black but soon to be yellow...ones and twos still to fall.... Yes, light was infiltrating from the south. Again she notices the flies on the water, flies finer than dust. Winter wasn't doing its job but everything now is backwards.

The old man had told her about the slacks freezing. Frost on the ice, on its rutted scrim and how that ice had groaned beneath his feet. He described crouching to peer into its astigmatic glooms and seen the weeds waving. A girl's hair, he'd said. And ruffled her spikes.

When she'd spun away.

Can't a man touch? Can't a man touch his own...

But she'd made that gesture. Of dismissal. And now regretted it. Her hair was pink then. Said it all.... In her snakebite days. Back room of the Buck days. Tough cookie? Hardly. But knew enough not to walk home alone. Through the fairground dark, its stanchions creaking. Well, girl, you do it now. And today the waves are breaking over the pub, an ocean rising higher than the karaoke machine...

No, the old man had never helped. But in the barn his library rewarded exploration. Those notebook pages were a kind of autobiography. Yet what could anyone believe?

She understood there was a time before the sand. Before the sand covered the Neolithic fields, small as quillets, the old man had said. Pushing the word down her throat. He'd seen fields like that in Ireland, he said. Yeah, well...

Now here was colour. Those sea buckthorn berries....
She and the others had once tried to make buckthorn chut-
ney using the fruits with marrows from an abandoned
allotment. They'd allowed it to ferment and someone had
been sick, sipping too much of the potcheen. They're great
for vitamin C, she had told them. They....

Both deer drank a long time. Good sign, she thought.
The sea had broken through in the south and there was a
blow-out reaching from the beach one hundred yards into
the sand hills. A salt lagoon had formed. That coastal path
was... nowhere. But it had never felt real.

She couldn't go round the freshwater slack without
immersing herself. The pools were greater now, and every
hollow a mangrove swamp. She's seen her brother swim in
these dunes, freshwater from the emergences meeting salt
from the tides. No longer a border between the sweet and
the.... All was confusion. What had worked before no longer
applied.

The dunes were unrecognizable. Some of the willows
stood in ten feet of water. They had grown through the
scree left after sand mining. Every dipwell had vanished.
The dunes she'd known were gone. Everything was lost or
rearranged by the new tides. Or by the hurricanes. Yet it
was nothing new.

4.
Remember Riley? she asked herself. Riley had excavated
every tumulus, Pwll Swil included. Meticulous? Yes, grain

by grain. And what had Riley found? Graves beneath cap-stones, children's bones pointing south, pointing west. What did that mean, she wondered.

Nothing now. Even meaning was warped today. Time was different. But Riley's notes had instructed historians on burial of the dead. And the dead were young. Always young...

Cuttlebone?
Goatwillowstick?
Jay's feather in a purse?

That's what those children in the dune had left behind. With a few flint flakes. But how often had she placed her ear to the sand and listened. *And listened....* As she was doing now below the smashed tumulus, froth in the waves at its foot. Yes, think of the children who loved this place because they knew no other.

Scour her skull, the sand will.

Leave her pelvis a white saddle.

Whose hips broad, whose hips barren?

No children would reveal those bones of her dreaming. And the crack in her collarbone, healed as a scar? She'd seen the X-ray like a crucifix in the dark.

And here she is now: a shadow on the pool.

Steelies scuffed raw. Czech army surplus olive green thermal socks. And oh the rest of it, the rest of it...

Yes, she could hear the stream coming from the spring. They'd recorded that, her and her brother, and put a drone track over it, something she invented, a long note that only changed three times, up an octave, and down, and playing over that her voice, her whispering, her beatboxing of that graffito that might still be there, *Save U, Save U...* repeated one hundred times...

Maybe it was meant to be *Save Us*, but the woman thought her way was best, with her own chords above the drone, above the stream, and for percussion her own breath, her own breath.... Put together in the barn and to be heard after her time. By...?

But when it's ready, she asks herself, why not broadcast as loudly as possible? Like the foghorn she remembers down the coast, that white trumpet they'd started using again, years after it had last sounded. Speaking of emergency. The voice of the past angry with the present.... Too late, ladies and gentlemen, but *Save U, Save U...*

Yeah, that was history but what did it mean? Every man for himself? It was the old man himself who had shown her the words, sprayed on the valences as he called them, the army firing ranges from way back. What had he said? *Back in the day*. But it had not been his day, ever.... So, dark concrete, white paint. *Save U?* The old man had shrugged. And given his mysterious smile.

He was showing his age by then. The knees had gone. Perhaps his mind. The next week another tempest had blown in. Maybe that was when they started using the fog-horn again.... Last resort for the last resort.

She crosses to a gravel bank left over from mining, willow pushing through, and rags of rosebay like the old man's hair....

In her palm an oyster shell, its mother of pearl. She glances up, then around. Almost marooned, she thinks. But isn't everyone now?

Okay, an hour of soft sand, but try the climb. Get the whole panorama up there. Take an hour in this weird light but climb into the spindle wood that her brother called fire trees. Maybe that's where the deer have gone.

Yes, take an hour. Remember all the hiding places along the way. That's how she thinks these days. Of somewhere to be safe. But she'd get an idea, just an idea and see the changes. If the dogs don't scatter her first...

In Tom Briton's Country

On the Set of *Lawrence of Arabia* in Tom Briton's Country: SS 85552 77080

1.
what the sand conceals
is not what the sand reveals

...area of drifting...
walls...wells...an ancient road
walls...wells...an ancient road

flint implements and arrow heads
found AD 1897...

Black Rocks...
Low water mark

...walls
  wells...

…an ancient road
…walls…wells…an ancient road
...area of drifting…
…high water mark of ordinary tides…
…Tower (remains of)

2.

And there, no *there,* sanderlings where the waves break, 7 of them in step.

Maybe their symmetry is prayer. And surely celebration.

Perhaps they will teach me to dance, these sanderlings, always in prime numbers, 3, 7, 11 as I muse on marine mathematics.

Yes 17 on the shore but now 19 is surely the answer, no, now 31 these 43 these 57 surely the answer as I work out the square root of sanderlings.

3.

But what the sand reveals is not all that the sand conceals

Unrecorded…unclassified…these places…
remains of…walls…wells…an ancient road
walls…wells…an ancient road.

And at night a commote of stars with Mars red as a pheasant's eye reflected in Pwll y Briton Tom

Yet I know I will wake one day I will wake unrecorded and unclassified and I'll find myself counting to one *hwndrwd*... here, in Tom Briton's country.

4.

Oh!

How are you, Mr O Toole? I ask quickly. (Yet it might be Omar Sharif).

Epic, he replies.

But tell me, where can a man find a drink in this desert?

He is wearing a scarlet bisht and holding a bone-handled shafra, gazing down from the tor, neat as a goshawk on the imperial wrist.

So, I look around: And am puzzled. Sand to the horizon both east and west and the wayfarer's tree splendid as an honour guard.

Two miles, I say, *to the Ancient Briton. Two miles to the Pelican in her Piety.*

And now he comes sideways down that golden escalator and heads east, maybe looking askance at my irrepressible native insouciance.

5.

Cooler, it grows cooler. But here's... *hemlock* – a hollow haulm bending in the rain.

Soon its stem will rattle and darkness fall.

But for now as tall as I, this horse poisoner.
Surely Socrates knew what was in the bowl?
He sipped in scorn, proud and disbelieving.
The spotted viper is no kinder...

6.
undefined...
        unrecorded...
                unclassified...
these places...
remains of...

and I'm counting to one *hwndrwd*
until I wake unrecorded unclassified

in an area of drifting...

At night this commote of stars and Mars red as a pheasant's
eye reflected in...

  ...Drift...
    Driftwood...
    Drifting...

7.
    One last thing, calls O'Toole from a summit. (But increas-
ingly he resembles Omar Sharif). *Where did Riley dig?*
    I look around. Not far from where you're standing, I reply.

And that famous photograph? I ask. Have you seen it?
Who hasn't? he calls. *Part of my homework.*
And he sets off. But south this time.

Musketeers, I hear him call. *Rehearsing here for god knows
what unholy war.*
But bones first of all. Bones under stones.
Because William Riley had excavated a tumulus in 1905.
Approximately...*here.* Yes, Riley in pith helmet like an
African explorer, discovering a sarcophagus. Digging into
legend...

8.
Is what these sands reveal
all that these sands conceal?

This is saltwort, caustic, where we build our fire, and I sleep
rolled in a blanket beside it, a brand that shifts in the beach
breeze, its shadow under Alpheratz, my mother's star –
tonight blue as driftwood ash – and I feel its roots in the
bedrock, the limestone that allows...

walls, wells,
an ancient road...

walls
wells
and an ancient road...

Alleged Autobiography of a Sowerby's Beaked-Nose Whale, found near Sker, south Wales

I rose thousands of feet. A legend that then lowered itself into a limestone vice.

When washed ashore a tractor hauled me down the dram road to be rendered. My flukes, my ingots of fat, the green and goosebeaked rostrum: even my pale lice running out of the sun, whalelice skedaddling over Sker, the gulls, in pennants on the sea, at last abandoning their prosecution.

Wild, this whale. Perplexed by parasites. Or the brine in my brainpan.

At eleven tons only a stripling, yet a secret stranger. And unchronicled.

No page apparatus in the encyclopaedias – as if I was waiting for the world to catch up.

Yet did I dream a boy carving his name into my vast and velvet hull?

Red Magpies at Bwlch y Cariad

Head Name	Undefined
Type	Unclassified
Grid Reference	SS 84089 77236
Parish	Newton Nottage
County	Glamorgan
When recorded	1898-1908
Primary Source	*OS 2nd Edition Maps*
Secondary Source	*Great Britain 1900 website*
Notes	Imported from GB1900

… fel claret yw ei lliw mwyaf cyffredin, fel pe buasai wedi golchi ei gwisg mewn gwin, a'd dillad yng ngwaed y grawnwin. Dyna liw ei chefn, a'i gwddw. Rhed rhimyn llydan o ddu, un ffunud a mwstash—mwstash ymherodrol – o fôn y big i hanner y gwddw. Brith yw ei chap fel gwasgod Bronfraith, gydag adlewyrchiadau porffor. Tywyll yw'r gynffon, eithr purwyn fel ôd…
Twm o'r Nant

Banditos?

A pair fly up together but which is which?

Pink, I'd say, or claret-in-water, a white rump, a purple sheen. These dandies, both with black imperial moustache and speckled crown, mock anyone left behind. Or less grand.

They remind me of the Albanians who waved goodbye in Durazzo. Lean and dangerous, weapons concealed.

Yes, this is the ju-ju of jays as they leave me scanning empty air. Their syllables are scorn, Gwenhwyseg guttural-ogy ancient as history, keeping the secret and the power that secret brings of the divine right of jays.

Because jays are born to it, yes jays are born to it – but this acre they own is our lost empire – while jays are only jealous of that jewel hidden in their wings…

The Riders at Pwll y Briton Tom

Head Name	Undefined
Type	Unclassified
Grid Reference	SS 85552 77080
Parish	Merthyr Mawr
County	Glamorgan
When recorded	1898-1908
Primary Source	*OS 2nd Edition Maps*
Secondary Source	*Great Britain 1900 website*
Notes	Imported from GB1900

I have heard them before I hear them because I have always heard them, hoof echoing hoof, proof echoing proof… these horses' hooves, still sudden on the sand.

But what stirs in me? Not ancient blood but an avatar that will always be my dark companion. Wearily familiar ghost.

The riders are invisible riders… horses shod, unshod upon Traeth yr Afon, hoof echoing hoof, proof echoing proof….

Yes, what stirs in me is the footsoldier's fear, my horseless tribe at war without weapons and fearful of iron, dreadful iron, the fierce art and alchemy of the forge forgone or forgotten or never fostered by our people.

Yet in my head, every footfall – huge and hollow – must foretell... our future.

So I fight with all I possess, the Silurian magicians' torc of woven names for the constellations repeated as a spell over and over, an incantation in a language soon to be lost, as if my own heart was beating beneath the sand, while in this chill the unknown riders pass, quick as meteors, hoof echoing hoof proof echoing proof... the sound of a host, these riders who must, who will follow me forever...

Wearily familiar ghost...

Burning the Sunflowers

1.

Winter, we kept the seeds in vanilla envelopes, trusting they'd stay dry. And yes, we planted sunflower seeds, those white triangles like babies' teeth, and some failed and others never showed at all and others we transplanted, but these we watched grow tall and higher than either of us, an avenue I stood within at dusk, my face amongst their faces, darkness crawling in my veins, October's moon rolling around on the dunes.

2.

Smouldering all night this fire, green on the outside, hardly singed, but hidden within, a pyramid of ash.

I had split the trunks with a spade, those hollow stems soon smoking that were long as didgeridoos.

And how like us I think are sunflowers, some still standing although there's nothing left, and now in ruination these sunflower bones are incandescent in the ash, a flame in every honeycomb smaller than the seed from which each came.

3.

Some have no truck with sunflowers, thinking them water hoarders, but soon relays of fire run from one crown to the next, last petals yellow as the dynamite dust my mother brushed away at the Ordnance, while lit from the tinderbox I think of those flames crawling through the night unseen, crowns consumed with all the royal rags while scattered here these seeds I'll keep next year, my mouth to the fire giving the kiss of life.

Lizards

Are making a comeback, the weather enticing them out.

Yes, this the best summer I can remember for lizards, their throats pulsing, and acid yellow, the lizards' undersides, those queens of the ochre pit.

I know the tracks such lizards leave, footprints faint in the sand, finer than any bird, the sandgrains hardly disturbed.

Vipers also. There was an adder on the path last week, diamonds dark on its back, almost black, that viper. Black is their tribal colour. Our local strain of basilisks.

Adders were always black in these dunes. But I recall, years ago, one with its zigzags yellow as gorse petals.

At my feet, in toxic somnolence, that serpent had lain, its cold coil strange as a fossil one step away.

But all such creatures are returning as the sunlight persists. As if a debt is being paid to the chill of reptilia.

Golden Plover at Ffynnon Wen

Orwell wrote 'vilely cold', and there was frost on my car,
but by afternoon I was piling turf and scrubbing hands in
the rain barrel.

Now in the quartz of Ffynnon Wen I discover a plover
not yet in its gold corslet but single, stunned and considering its own death.

Those matches I borrowed didn't strike on limestone so I
begged his Dunhill from Em, one allotment up.

Soon the *Express* had caught, and my tinder teased from
sunflower dust and tips of raspberry canes had taken.

Yes, I've been burning the ghosts of the sunflowers,
blackened as old bones they, the rootballs of the sunnies
fistsized.

Another season soon follows the sunflowers and I carried
Emlyn's canes with an armful of sticks and rearranged the
glossy charcoal the wood had become, twice burning my
hand and when I walked away there were sparks at my toe,

and I ask Em to guard the fire although I knew it was out,
and tonight I'm back to 1984 remembering The Party held
that stars are fragments of fire a few kilometres distant, and
perhaps I might have believed it and posted something on
Face Book as now I'm blaming melt in the Arctic for this
evening ironclad.

Snipe, Vanishing

OS six-inch to the mile 1888-1913

Head Name	Undefined
Type	Unclassified
Grid Reference	SS 85705 76884
Parish	Merthyr Mawr
County	Glamorgan
When recorded	1898-1908
Primary Source	*OS 2nd Edition Maps*
Secondary Source	*Great Britain 1900 website*

Yes, a stuttering song from the marsh goat, its zigzaggery over the dune slack.

But it's already hard to believe it was ever here. Snipe are more difficult to follow than a knight on a chessboard.

It's gone like a thought, so rare it has become in the human mind. And one day we will wake from our dreams of extinction and hear the child in us groan like an old man denying such a creature has ever flown.

Because there never was a lake and there never was a dune... and this is a book of ghosts, reader. Only a book of ghosts...

Schwyll: The Great Spring of Glamorgan

I Dduw rho glod am ddwr glan

1.

On the oldest map I can find: walls and wells and ancient roads, walls and wells, whilst Schwyll begins as a bud and becomes a berry, its water first a rice grain then white as a rice flower, yes here, the fountainhead, source of anti-thirst, each drop from the honeycomb, this chalk pocked with resurgences, winter pools and godless wells, yet all these wells are worshipful, their swallets in the swale as the Great Spring sweats from Schwyll into Pwll Swil.

2.

Mother, I have dug my fingers into the sand and felt only the ash of my father's crematorium urn that twenty-five years ago you hid behind the catfood tins.

This summer so dry – as if water had been banished for millennia!

Walls and wells and ancient roads, walls and wells and ancient roads, then here, at the wellspring, the fountainhead on the oldest map I can find.

Is there a tachograph for water? A black box? The pumping station that we find has become a museum, its lexicon archaic, yet the Great Spring seeps from its limestone lagoons.

Six million gallons they say of sweetwater, today, tomorrow and through the generations – as if there is a glacier down there, thawing in secret…

Fellow Travellers

Fellow Travellers

(for Jan Morris)

1. Hay: Thomas Peregrine, Ty Mawr

Hallucination, wasn't it? Or a dream of summer.

But look, that's nothing to do with it. That's nothing to do with it at all...

No, it's something about the bales in Cae Morfa, red with dock and clover.

That rick was a city built by pitchfork as I climbed its perfumed escalator with haydust moustache, harvestmen, raw tails of the rats.

That day Peregrine had spoken.

Beware the stammerer's weed, he said, though I was eager only for a snort of stone ginger.

For him, the grass had been dry two months, and look, there it was, horsepoisoner, queen of the rags.

Yet who was Peregrine? I grew up beside him, one of those Iberians dark as dogwood, and as hard, for some, to stomach.

Mould grew on his overcoat, and when he decided he'd had enough, he tied the sleeves together.

Someone found him on Christmas morning, frost in the straw, shins yellow as elder sticks.

Thomas Peregrine, who lived behind a stile, limped, and said nothing is more beautiful than a cow's eyelashes.

That brazier he cut to hold head-high might scar the liver, and soon after coma comes death, he said. Be it slow.

And it's only now when I breathe the bales again, brown and silver like a burnt book, that Peregrine returns, extinct as are all that tribe yet alive in this air for one moment of the ghost-harvest.

What he'd seen in his old man's life might have meant something, surely?

Last, he had said, find a pebble to suck if it's words that irk you. Meaning me and no other as I slid, rubbing my eyes and spitting, out of the hay…

2. Bedouin Children

encountered near Israel/Jordan's Dead Sea

Bedouin children of a one camel clan say *ay meester,* say *geev munn-nee.*

Bedouin children of a one camel clan are instructed that God is within them and not within them.

Bedouin children of a one camel clan tighten a lorry's fan-belt on a slope of an extinct volcano on a shore of a prehistoric sea.

Bedouin children of a one camel clan squat and bury their scat like the caracal.

Bedouin children of a one camel clan bleed barefoot in the flints and flinders on a slope of an extinct volcano on a shore of a prehistoric sea.

Bedouin children of a one camel clan bathe in sand and ashes, ashes and sand.

Ronaldinho and *Ronaldo* on their football shirts have faded to starlight in the desert dark.

But Bedouin children of a one camel clan are instructed that God is within them and not within them.

And Bedouin children of a one camel clan say *ay meester,* say *geev munn-nee…*

3. 'Tiano: El Risco, Sicily

You are the first people I've met here, said 'Tiano, to speak our language. So many give more time to our dogs.

He had come along the path carrying a papaya in a bucket, old gold as a Wolves shirt, that fruit.

Then he pointed to the pine tree where his brother, catching rabbits, fell with a heart attack.

So we split it for breakfast, skin too and those peppery seeds, and promised when we returned not to discuss foreign weather.

It's the people, 'Tiano says. Never the sun. Which is true. Yet I've talked continually of the sky over El Risco because as I came through the cane, dead fronds underfoot, there they were, the Moorish stars.

I've always found them impossible as prickly pears in the mouth, Alpheratz, Mizar and Beetlejuice, bloody that one least of all on my tongue.

Yes, navigating, I'd discovered Aldebaran, red as a coffee bean, or the pomegranates that lie in January under the trees in Finca La Laja.

South I thought so south I sought…

4. Girl in Valletta

I watch, her hair intricate as a wren's nest,
hands wrapped in some sea creature's skin.

This girl slices salami thinner than a contact lens,
pulls her cheesewire through Mediterranean towns.

Look how their walls are now separated
by irrefutable light.

So I wait with my ticket and there are thousands
ahead of me and thousands and thousands behind, a
few grapes on the counter for us to taste, a cup to spit
our olive stones.

And I think, if there was a cup for our words
it would be as huge as a warehouse or an iron box
with a hundred silver clasps.

Then, after a long time, my number is called,
and she is looking without seeing into my face.

This girl who is angry, this girl in her bloody chemise.

5. Kelly Jones, Sydney: A Day and Night in the Raw Republic

Any Welsh in tonight? .....
Any Irish? .....
Any fuckin Australians?

(Kelly Jones, The Stereophonics, outdoor free concert, Sydney, April 18, 2010.)

The fruit bats cruise over the stage where the band sits but Kelly Jones doesn't ask if there are fruit bats in tonight.

Kelly Jones doesn't understand fruit bats. Kelly Jones doesn't see fruit bats. Kelly Jones is not DH Lawrence although they are about the same size, spare as sparrow-hawks.

And Kelly Jones doesn't ask if David Herbert Lawrence is in this evening, beneath the gum trees, in the indigo dusk, gliding over the stage, or hanging upside down as fruit bats hang. Kelly Jones does not have sequin eyes or a nectar nibbling tongue.

Now the sky turns the colour of oxy acetylene. But Kelly Jones does not change key.

6. At the Bronx Zoo

(for Gerrie Clancy)

I think I've seen it somewhere before, in the subway or the park maybe, on a bench as the twilight brings out the black dyslexic neon over our faces, its eyes flickering there like a lover's tongue.

And later at some street corner hunched against the wall, eyes squeezed shut this time, face to the floor, and the hand outstretched as if it held a trophy, the white plastic cup with its foam of crushed dollars.

Out of its canyon the long cat slides, flexing a bronze knuckle over the stone of the Bronx. The leaves, fallen, are the shapes of its footprints, that pulse of neon the marbling in its eye.

7. Jean Marie de Moissac, Biggar, Saskatchewan: Wild Swimming

Early May on a cold day. Snow like lines of barbed wire. Between Biggar and Perdue, a gravel trail off a quiet road. But she is busy with farm work, a farm that doesn't have a name. They grow canola there and sometimes plough the prairie. Her husband drives a Dodge Dakota pickup with a cracked windscreen. All the pick ups I ever see in Saskatchewan have cracked windscreens.

I ask her if she swims but she is talking about prairie sage and the pasque flower and how she and her woman friends take their bloodied rags at night into the prairie for burial. Had to be deep enough to prevent coyotes.... Ritual magic, I supposed.

Farm woman, poet with a story in *Playgirl*, and no, she says, she doesn't swim in the farm's lake. Not there. Not ever. It's a soda lake. You don't have soda lakes? There are plenty in the province. Maybe they've always been here, or perhaps they're more recent. And no, the lake doesn't have a name that she knows. Or a name that the Woodland Cree have told her. Yes, she ought to ask.... She imagines it's on the map, being pretty big.

As it is chilly she gives me a sheepskin and I keep on my old school scarf. I used it more in the province than any-where.... Sentimental, I suppose, about its ancient stripes. I never wore it at school.

Yet come to think, she says, other people swim. I've heard too that sometimes the government releases pickerel fry. But they never last long.

She also says one night she'd seen a meteor shower like that fire in the Ukrainian church that filled the western sky. Drinkers in the Perdue Hotel had stood on their pick up roofs, gesturing at the fat bushels of sparks...

Three years later I am in Baghdad where all the cars have cracked windscreens and are kept running by ingenious Iraqi mechanics. The only other cars seem to be black Mercedes owned by members of the Ba'ath party. All are parked illegally at a conference I am trying to film. Saddam, I note, hasn't arrived yet...

8. Marwhan Makhoul at Zichon Yakhouv – Golan

(after his Arabic)

Marwan Makhoul wrote of the Golan Heights, where clouds are more fortunate than exiles. They might return to the summits as snow.But the villages are vacant and his Golan only ghosts.

Now the drones whine like children in the dark whilst the sea is black as surgical stitch, a surf sound in Jaffa this morning, and I hear the same surf in Haifa tonight.

There are watchmen on Golan and also the watchers of Golan, but the restless children must sit under the tables whilst the babies are shut into drawers.

Yes, Golan is young, whose oleanders are locked like lovers in its dry riverbeds. So many generations have passed that death holds no dismay. Yes, Golan has always been young.

And they learn the predator's sigh, the voice of the reaper. Over the ghettoes of Gaza comes the harpies' music, while in the ruined boulevards a child is weeping.

So many prayers but all are prey. Ah, ghosts of Golan, says Marwan Makhoul, one final time. I visited you when stars shone like candlelit windows on your slopes. But it was your festivals that brought me back, and not grief's guilt. I know how memories maim.

Now over the ghettoes comes the harpies' music. So many prayers but all is prey. Yet, it is right to think like this, seeing Damascus in the distance, and its dust drifting like dreams of great poetry or a feast for a returning son.

But now over the ghettoes comes the harpies' music, the predator's sigh, the reaper's voice. And the children still cry all night.

DU: Screenshots from a film concerning 'The Mother of All Battles, Iraq, 1991…'

1. Beatrice

Team leader.
On the flight to Amman I note she is reading
The Protocols of the Elders of Zion.
Oh, I think.
Then return to *Rolling Stone.*

2. Abu Nuwas

There is a street named after him and the statue we film shows
the poet still joined to his cup. One of Baghdad's special bards….
So, with arak we toast Abu Nuwas, wine-worshiper, roisterer in
chief. But the boys he adored were beardless and we wonder what
now is allowed….

3. Mohammed Ghani

A gentle soul. We tour his studio in a reek of solder and thinners. But once Ghani took an impression of Saddam's thumb and used it in the great Victory arch…

Hah, I ask.

As in every Devil's Museum around the world?

Where the devil's thumbprint is burnt into to his vodka glass? But how else might an artist live…?

4. Public Shelter 25

When the four hundred and eight became aware, every exit was sealed, they climbed upon one another's shoulders, babies the summit of the pyramid.

I thought they were moths but when Nazaar directed the torch and pointed our camera such creatures became hands fused to the cement.

All that was left when the bodies were pulled away was a grey clinker leaving 816 black hands on the ceilings of Amiriya.

Gradually I realise people are looking at me.

Time slows down. At last I am forced to wonder why those people are not tearing me apart…

5. Procession Street, Babylon

Exploring alone I come upon the lion of Babylon with its curious basalt smile. After nearly three thousand years I see it now in the weeds, sand covering its pedestal.

We are not unlike he slave it devours, an Assyrian snared in the grass, that sacrificial child by death defiled.

Saddam of course, designed a tank called the Lion of Babylon but nightblind, squat, it never fired a shot...

6. Tower of Babel

The boy tells me what I want to hear. So, this is where it stood, the mudbrick foundation of surrealism.

And I listen to the tide in the Tigris and then the washerwomen who sing whilst tamping their children's clothes.

Every syllable different and unrepeatable. And I learn, yes, Babel was only a columbarium for words...

7. Jumhiriya Bridge

... out alone again, team leader back at the hotel, divvying up what we owe our guide: dollars, royal Jordanian pounds, our last sterling, all scrambled together with the medicines we've smuggled, in a heap on her bed.

And on the Jumhiriya bridge I meet an old man, smiling at his own destitution as I pass him one of Saddam's dirty banknotes, fifty almost worthless dinars, on a bridge that one side or the other will soon destroy.

I never understood why they hated each other so much.

And a man comes up and in perfect English says, no, we never knew beggary in Baghdad. Not for a thousand years.

8. North Gate Cemetery, Waziriah, Baghdad

Directly above us, the Water Bearer, and then the Swallower.

Yet despite the countless draughts under Aquarian stars there is no well deeper than arak...

Cholera is a filthy death. At the North Gate lie so many who died the same way, men and officers, because an epidemic does not discriminate....

But someone must have swept the sand away and picked the litter left by arak-drinkers, thin men with black blisters on their lips, bottles recycled until the plastic was worn out by arak acid.

Yes, despite the countless draughts under Aquarian stars there is no well deeper than arak. What fools, you'd say, of those who dare their own delirium?

Delicious and deliberate, those pearls for which they drowse and drown, molten tears amongst the white headstones, once bottle-strewn.

Sots with the staggers, or disciples together at the last stupor? But despite the countless draughts under Aquarian stars there is no well deeper than arak...

Such care must have been taken before we examined the graves. But sand? I know its needles on Traeth yr Afon and understand it finds us out, as it did these soldiers in the North Gate, men who died off the map, but were hauled here first, John Somebody, John Nobody, defeat and victory both ending with sand, with the crack of palms, and arak

so strong it might steal the breath, its burn on the tongue a
different kind of thirst.

9. The Sewer

Above our heads lies the jewellery district which means
there are prospectors in these tunnels searching for gold.

No-one knows me here. And nowhere is stranger than
this where a thousand gutters spill and I pause on the top
rung before climbing down to the lake, the glittering velvet
of the desert sky, to join the men in masks and bandanas,
some barechested, most in rags, unpaid, unafraid, this
handful who hold the city on their shoulders...

10. Scherezade

The dollars are gone, only dinars left. I too will leave Baghdad destitute.

Every morning the chambermaid in her heartbreak-
ing uniform looks at the camera recharging by the hotel's
erratic electricity.

I press on her the last of the asprins and think maybe I
should play her the interview filmed yesterday at the Min-
istry for Information. But it will tell her nothing she does
not already know...

11. Checkpoint, Iraq-Jordan border

My atlas tells me *Badiet esh Sham* but *black* is the word for
this obsidian field, a layer of pumice, its light locked away.

But in one window of the bus, a Mesopotamian moon and when I turn my head to the other half of the sky I try counting the sprawl of Arabian stars, that hemisphere my tongue might whisper, an impossible secret known only to myself as if I am the discoverer, the first someone, yes, surely the first, the first and only to gaze at Algol, the demon, the ghoul that would strike any child of Babylon blind as a stone, one of the creatures I would meet on Procession Street behind the Ishtar Gate, my camera with its shuttered eye riding with me, yet sleeping, maybe dreaming as I am dreaming of what I have seen and what is to come, that camera bandaged now like an invalid in the rags of my shirt...

Acknowledgements

Some of *Delirium* has appeared elsewhere, sometimes in different forms.

I'd like to thank the editors of *New Welsh Review*, *The Lonely Crowd*, *PN Review*, *Long Poem Magazine*, *Poetry Wales*, Manchester Metropolitan University's on-line Covid19 project.

Also Daniel Robicheau and Beatrice Boctor for their invitation to help make a film about depleted uranium.

Also Alexandra Buchler for invitations from 'Literature Across Frontiers' to Israel, Malta and India.

Thanks also to Marwan Makhoul, from whose Arabic I have made an expanded version of his 'Golan'.

Also Dan Llywelyn Hall for his idea for our joint creation of 'The Dunes', (2019), and for permission to use 'Schwyll (sic) – The Great Spring of Glamorgan' as cover art.

The pieces from 'Billionaires' Shortbread' are part of a work-in-progress. Ultimately this will follow four characters.

'In Tom Briton's Country' is based on real places in Merthyr Mawr dunes, near Porthcawl, namely Twmpath Briton Tom and Pwll y Briton Tom. 'Hwndrwd' from 'Tir y Hwndrwrd' – the name of the local commote. All place names are factual and all ordnance survey references correct to the best of my knowledge. Sand dune scenes were filmed there for the film 'Lawrence of Arabia', director David Lean, 1962. Gwenhwyseg (p.122) is the dialect of Welsh formerly spoken in south-east Wales.

The Author

Robert Minhinnick is a multi-prizewinning poet, essayist and novelist. His most recent poetry collection, 'Diary of the Last Man', was shortlisted for the TS Eliot Prize in 2017 and won Wales Book of the Year, which he has now won three times. Two of his novels, 'Sea Holly' and 'Nia', were shortlisted for the RSL Ondaatje Prize. He edited the leading poetry magazine 'Poetry Wales' for ten years, and continues to champion and enable new writers.

Minhinnick is a founder of Friends of the Earth Cymru and of Sustainable Wales, and has written extensively on the environment. In 2021 he edited 'Gorwelion: Shared Horizons', a book of essays on climate change.

He was awarded a prestigious Hay Festival Medal in 2022.